PRAISE FOR *GO...*

My friend Ken Costa, in his book *God ...*
life-changing steps to live out your fai... ...ng g... ...
God. Outside of your marriage and family, God uses work as a school
for character development. You'll experience tremendous joy in letting
God work in you and through you at work.

—RICK WARREN
PASTOR, SADDLEBACK CHURCH,
AND AUTHOR OF INTERNATIONAL
BESTSELLER, *The Purpose Driven Life*

I can think of few people better qualified to write on the subject of
faith in the workplace than my friend Ken Costa. His strong Christian
faith and his skills in the world of finance mean that he has had to do
what he writes about. I commend this book very warmly.

—JUSTIN WELBY
ARCHBISHOP OF CANTERBURY

No one is better qualified than Ken Costa to write a book like this.
Throughout his rise to one of the most senior positions in the banking
world, he has been an inspiration to countless Christians seeking to
live out their faith in their workplaces. Ken and I met at Cambridge
University, where we both became Christians. He has been one of my
closest friends ever since. I am so glad he has been persuaded at last to
put some of his wisdom and experience into print.

—NICKY GUMBEL
VICAR OF HTB, LONDON, AND
PIONEER OF THE ALPHA COURSE

Packed with wisdom and practical advice for the workplace—this
book will inspire, stretch, and challenge you.

—STEVE CHALKE
FOUNDER OF OASIS GLOBAL AND FAITHWORKS

Ken Costa is one of the outstanding bankers of his generation, who is known for the passion, creativity, leadership, and strategic thinking that he brings to his professional life. He is also a person of a deep Christian faith, which comes out on almost every page of this book. *God at Work* is an extraordinary account of his own personal struggles with ambition, money, relationships, success, and failure. Integrating faith and work is a challenge for anyone in business, and I have no doubt that this book could transform the way you work.

—LORD GRIFFITHS OF FFORESTFACH
VICE-CHAIRMAN, GOLDMAN
SACHS INTERNATIONAL

In these pages, Ken Costa brings to bear the experience of a varied and highly responsible professional life so as to show just how the transforming gospel is at work in the workplace. It is full of acumen, shrewdness, hopefulness—in short, it is a wise book, and a delight and profit to read.

—ROWAN WILLIAMS
FORMER ARCHBISHOP OF CANTERBURY

God at Work goes a long way in pulling down the barriers that exist between the sacred and the secular. Ken's wide experience, from his theological training and Christian service at HTB and the Alpha program, to his success in the world of finance, makes him well qualified to write on the subject.

Can a Christian be fulfilled serving in the marketplace? How do "worldly" ideals of money, success, ambition, and power sit side by side with Christian virtues of love, justice, compassion, and service to God?

For anyone who has sought answers to these issues or anyone who has wondered how the Christian faith can thrive in a capitalist, market-driven workplace, this book is a must-read.

—PASTOR AGU IRUKWU
SENIOR PASTOR, JESUS HOUSE
FOR ALL NATIONS, LONDON

GOD AT WORK

LIVE EACH DAY WITH PURPOSE

KEN COSTA

W Publishing Group

An Imprint of Thomas Nelson

Published in Nashville, Tennessee, by W Publishing, an imprint of Thomas
Nelson. W Publishing and Thomas Nelson are registered trademarks of
HarperCollins Christian Publishing, Inc.

Thomas Nelson titles may be purchased in bulk for educational, business,
fund-raising, or sales promotional use. For information, please e-mail
SpecialMarkets@ThomasNelson.com.

Unless otherwise noted, Scripture quotations taken from the Holy Bible,
New International Version, copyright © 1973, 1978, 1984 International
Bible Society. Used by permission of Hodder & Stoughton, a member of
the Hodder Headline Group. All rights reserved. NIV is a trademark of
International Bible Society. UK trademark number 1448790. Scripture
marked 'The Message' is taken from The Message. Copyright © by Eugene
H. Peterson 1993, 1994, 1995, 1996, 2000, 2001, 2002. Used by permission
of NavPress Publishing Group. Scripture marked KJV is taken from The
Authorized (King James) Version. Rights in the Authorized Version are
vested in the Crown. Reproduced by permission of the Crown's patentee,
Cambridge University Press. The Holy Bible, Living Bible Edition, copyright
© Tyndale House Publishers 1971. All rights reserved. Scripture quotations
marked ESV are from The Holy Bible, English Standard Version˙ (ESV˙)
copyright © 2001 by Crossway, a publishing ministry of Good News
Publishers. All rights reserved.

**Library of Congress Cataloging-in-Publication Data is on
file with the publisher and the Library of Congress.**

ISBN 9780718087647

Printed in the United States of America

16 17 18 19 20 21 RRD 6 5 4 3 2 1

CONTENTS

INTRODUCTION

AS AN ACTIVE INVESTMENT BANKER AND FINANCIAL ADVISER IN THE city of London, I have read the *Financial Times* and the Bible almost every day for the last forty years. People often ask how I reconcile working in finance and being a Christian. There is a widespread view that God and business simply don't mix: the competitive, cutthroat demands of the marketplace are seen as the obvious enemy of Christian compassion and love. But I have found that the God who created and sustains the world is also the God of the workplace. If the Christian faith is not relevant in the workplace, it is not relevant at all. But where did this journey of faith start?

I was born in a nominally Christian country, South Africa, and grew up in the brutally oppressive apartheid era. From my early childhood I hated the fact that only white pupils could attend our school. I have never forgotten the day when we were told that the authorities had prevented children of color from receiving an education there. The injustice burns within me even now as I think back on it.

I became president of the Students' Union at university in Johannesburg and was active in the student protest movements against the so-called Christian doctrine of apartheid, whose warped theology laid claim to biblical authority for its most vicious consequences. The cruelty of the "separate but equal" philosophy provoked in me a burning sense of injustice. Black students were not allowed into the university or halls of residence, and every form of social intercourse was cut off. Offended by such injustices carried out in the name of Christianity, I became anaesthetized to the personal claims of Christ. I thus rejected Christianity in favor of what I considered the only effective philosophy of life, and the only one that would liberate people from the intolerable inhumanity of the apartheid system: Marx's "concept of man." In his book *Marx's Concept of Man*, Erich Fromm showed the way in which Marx outlined the path to freedom by stressing our common humanity, not merely our economic activities.

After completing a philosophy and law degree, I left South Africa because it had become clear to me that such resistance would never bring about peaceful change without a seismic change of heart. I continued my studies in England at the University of Cambridge. While there, I met a number of students whose lives had been changed during a Christian mission to the university. To this day they are among my best friends. Through them I came to see that at the center of the Christian faith there was not so much a system of thought, but rather a person, Jesus Christ, whose life, crucifixion, and resurrection had brought about the only true freedom that I or anyone would ever find. One evening, alone in my room, I read through the whole of Mark's gospel (because it was the shortest). I found both the claims and character of Christ compelling, and I saw in Jesus the "free-est" person who ever lived. Previously, I had heard only short sections of the Bible read at church services. The effect of reading the whole gospel in one sitting in a modern translation was electric. God was strangely one of us. I was struck by this picture of Christ as a human being who was committed to me. I therefore embraced the faith that I had grown up with but had hitherto neglected.

I realized that Christ alone, and no other philosophy, including that of Marx, could really change a person's life permanently through forgiveness and freedom. This faith came alive for me after an internal struggle as to whether God would be in charge of all my life, or only part of it. Many people accept just enough of Christianity to be miserable. I was in that camp. The struggle encapsulated itself in a vivid image of control drawn from the very marketplace where I would spend the next forty years: it was as if my life had shares and God wanted 100 percent control of it. A divine tug-of-war ensued. Why would God want all of me? Could there be a joint venture? Could I carve out a special deal to suit me? What about a partnership? Was 50/50 not a good arrangement? It became clear that true freedom was to be found in full surrender to the love of God. It did not come to me easily, nor at once: I got there in stages. I recall praying that God would take 51 percent of my life—control but not whole ownership.

I remember the churning and the heated deliberation within myself as this plan did not seem to achieve the desired objective. I saw then, and recognize now more fully, the arrogance of negotiating with God and the foolishness in believing I had anything to offer God. I recall praying: "Lord, have all of me. Only don't abandon me." In that moment, I realized that the God who loved the entire world also loved me and would stay faithful to me, even when I was not faithful to him, as has sadly often been the case.

What struck me at once was the immediate change in every area of my life. My internal wrestling on the meaning of life ceased, peace with God and with myself grew, and my life was redirected with a new passion. The Bible was suddenly filled with life and each week I read passages with a group of friends. I couldn't wait to attend these meetings. These readings laid the foundation for a dialectic that remains with me: drawing principles for living from the Bible, praying and talking them through with friends, and then applying them in practical day-to-day situations. But there was a nagging uncertainty. Did this all add up? Or were these experiences merely an enthusiastic response that would fizzle out and die? I decided to extend my full-time studies and read theology for a year to see whether the claims of Christianity could stand up to the rigors of academic examination. During this time I learned the grammar of the faith and found overwhelming evidence of the truth of Christ's claims to be God. Since then, I have never wobbled on the essential truth of the gospel story, although the implications have brought many questions and doubts. I also realized that theology was not merely a descriptive tool, useful in understanding the world better, but that the Christian task was to find God's way in the world and to work to change the world. I have been fired up by this challenge ever since.

Like many students leaving university, I felt overwhelmed by the prospect of choosing a career. There were just too many choices and too many questions about the purpose of work. I had read law and always assumed I would be a lawyer, yet increasingly I felt this might not be a good match for my personality, especially as I realized that I am not stimulated by detail. Having decided what not to do, the question of what to do remained. I knew that I could not work in South Africa, as I questioned the legitimacy of its government and I did not want to participate in an unjust economic system that had the tight restrictions of apartheid at its core. All I could do was put my talents to work and draw an unjustified reward, as the majority of the people would be excluded by reason of race from working in the same jobs. This discrimination left me deeply uneasy.

I therefore decided that I needed an overall framework to answer the question of whether the pursuit of profit was selfish or a true contribution to society. I came to realize that the New Testament was vigorously opposed to selfishness but clearly distinguished the possessive individualism of self-centeredness from self-interest. We are, after all, to love our neighbor as ourselves. I became convinced that democratic capitalism, despite its defects, was the economic system that served the common good and that best reflected the New Testament principles of justice, individual freedom, and responsible risk-taking.

Of course, over the years I have had my doubts about the

market economy. Sometimes it appears that the demand for efficiency unfairly discriminates against the weaker members of society. How can we justify the world becoming more efficient if it is more efficiently unfair? If the gap between the richest and the poorest widens year on year, something is clearly amiss. This particularly troubled me in recent times, when there seemed to be a headlong, compassionless pursuit of financial reward without restraint. At the start of the 2008 financial crisis, it became clear to me that free enterprise slipped its moral moorings. These considerations remain, but I have not found a better system. The market economy remains a good servant but a bad master—it needs to operate within a wider moral context that sees all human beings, and all the world's resources, as valuable, precisely because they matter to God. Without a values-based architecture, the market economy is weak in its foundations.

To be a Christian in this world today is therefore not comfortable. We will be challenged and left uneasy as we are prodded constantly by the Holy Spirit to question the ways in which the market economy serves the Christian objectives of justice and fairness. Our task is a distinctive one as we live our lives as witnesses of the Judeo-Christian values that undergird so much of the market economy.

These were the sorts of questions I struggled with as I made my career choice. I had an interview with a theological college and realized that theological training was not the route for me. A bishop even offered me a job, but there was no peace in my heart. As I thought, prayed, chatted to people, and visited the careers office, the banking and insurance industries started to emerge as the most promising possibilities. I therefore spoke to two friends working in those areas who were both older Christians and recent graduates, and who believed in the importance of faith at work. I decided to apply for jobs in both fields. I was rejected by three banks and two insurance companies, leaving me with a choice between one insurance company and one small merchant bank in London. I felt the responsibility of the choice before me affected not only me but any wife and family I might have in the future. I knew that God had plans for my life and that he was a party to the decision and not merely an observer. I prayed each day for God's guidance, reciting Psalm 37:5: "Commit your way to the LORD; trust in him and he will do this." I waited. There was no blinding light showing the path ahead but, instead, a growing conviction took hold of me that the banking door should be pushed first. I still felt sore about being rejected by the glamorous international banks, but nonetheless I accepted a London-based merchant banking job.

Merchant banks were the forerunners of investment banks: they are not high-street banks but financial institutions providing advisory, trading, and capital market services to sovereign governments and major financial institutions and corporations. Memorably, I started work on the day of a sterling crisis, when the pound was plummeting against the US dollar, and the government and the Bank of England were trying to halt the slide. I thus caught my first sight of the gripping fear and uncertainty that can dominate financial markets. At the time, a bemused colleague commented that, as nothing practical could avert the crisis, my theological training qualified me better than any of the panicking dealers. "You," he said, "can at least pray." So my career started.

Since then, I have prayed at work every day, almost without exception. I have tried to find time to pray at the start of the day, but often my prayers have been snatched between meetings or while traveling. I wish it weren't so, but the demands of the working day are not conducive to uninterrupted times of serene meditation. But these times, however imperfect, have equipped me for my work and reminded me daily of my reason for living and my dependence on God.

Living as a Christian in the world today is akin to living on a knife edge. Reading the Bible, praying, and talking to friends are all helpful, but there is no "click here" answer to the many dilemmas that we all face at work each day. A few years ago I went to the Namib Desert with a small group of Christian friends for a short break. For all of us, there was something quite captivating about the arid vastness of the landscape, its stark desolation, and its lack of distractions. In different ways, each one of us wanted to hear from God. We prayed and worshipped together and, at sunset one evening, surrounded by silence and the unforgettable darkness of Africa, we had a communion service under the stars on the sand. Next morning, we got up before sunrise to walk along one of the largest and most majestic sand dunes in the world. What we saw was remarkable. As the sun rose, on one side there was pure light; on the other, a still and eerie darkness. As I was walking along the top of the dune, I had the sense that this was a picture of the world in which Christians live. We are called to walk on the narrow ledge of the dune, not in darkness and not always in the sunlit beauty of the light side, but all the time leaning toward the light and away from the shadow.

The life of the Christian at work is a leaning toward goodness. Day by day we can sense God's presence as we avoid the darkness.

> "THE LIFE OF THE CHRISTIAN AT WORK IS A LEANING TOWARD GOODNESS."

We try to walk along this narrow divide, straining toward the light.

The workplace is a tough place but I have been encouraged by the belief that God has called us to be strengthened *in* the world *for* the world. This means embracing the challenges of a competitive world and growing through them in order to help others do the same. Knowing that each one of us has been placed in the world not by random accident but by God's design for a distinct purpose has carried me through many a difficult day.

During the last forty years, being a Christian at work has, if anything, become more difficult. In part, this is a response to the general angst of the world around us, from which no Christian is immune. Financial markets have become volatile, decisions more complex, and few choices are clear-cut. The global financial crisis of 2008–09 has heightened a palpable sense of uncertainty on a widespread scale—banks fearful of lending, entire countries facing economic ruin, and national banks being bailed out as a too-common occurrence. The harsh compromises that seem inevitable in the workplace have become more pressing as economic demands have grown.

It is clear to me that the biggest single contributor to the global financial crisis has been the breakdown of trust. The Bank of England's head of financial stability, Andy Haldane, said in September 2009: "It is lack of trust—and hence credit—that may shape the recovery."[1] More generally, in business, trust in CEOs and chairmen has plummeted. Shareholders, depositors, small businesses, and even regulators believe they have been let down. The economy has moved from one characterized by trust to one characterized by mistrust and suspicion. As risk has increased, trust levels have declined. Trusted professions and institutions have become less so. This has led to questions about where we get our authority from. We cannot merely rely on an increasing burden of regulations; rather we need to assert some common values. This breakdown of trust should challenge Christians in the workplace. What role do we, as Christians, have to play in reasserting the values of Christ in our workplaces?

The workplace is the coalface where faith is tested and sharpened by day-to-day encounters with the ambiguities and stresses of modern commerce. Our faith is tested when we recognize our weaknesses at work and learn more about our hard and soft spots in our working relationships, precisely because we cannot always choose the people with whom we work. We are tested and we interact—testily or graciously—with colleagues, or press our own selfishness ahead of the common good. Or we forget gratitude and miss God completely in the day-to-day frenzy of work. Each one of us has been there.

Some think that faith makes us immune from making wrong choices. I wish that were so. However, God does give us the spiritual resources to grow through our weaknesses and to recover when we succumb to the ever-present temptations we encounter in the workplace. The accusation of hypocrisy is the most hurtful. Others rightly expect those who embrace faith at work to act consistently with these values. We do not always do so. What I find hardest in others' judgment is that no allowance is made for the weakness that is common to us all. But I have come to appreciate each day not only the fellowship of believers to help and encourage, but also the critical—and not always helpful—reactions of colleagues. Through a combination of these I believe we grow into the rounded, well-adjusted human beings we are meant to be. None of us becomes a model of virtue instantly: life is lived out at work as part of a process, a learning experience. The greatest obstacle to maturing in our faith is ceasing to be teachable.

For the most part, I have had the privilege of hugely enjoying my work. In his book *Joy at Work*, Dennis Bakke, the former co-founder and chief executive of one of the largest energy companies in the world, discusses the ways in which "fun" became a core value of his company, in addition to the common principles of integrity, fairness, and social responsibility. His Christian faith led him to the view that "A joy-filled workplace gives people the freedom to use their talents and skills for the benefit of society, without being crushed or controlled by autocratic supervisors."[2] Yet many work without this element of joy. One of the purposes of this book is to explore ways of recovering it.

But there are moments when a sense of depression seems to hover over me at work. The causes are often deep-seated, but the triggers go off unexpectedly—a failed transaction, a disappointing pay review, unpleasant relationships, fear of the future. These times of trial happen to everyone. They are, however, opportunities for God to be glorified. The apostle Paul said, "When I am weak, then I am strong" (2 Corinthians 12:10). I have come to see that weakness is very hard to show in the workplace unless we remember its object is strength—our dependence on God.

No Christian truly comes of age until he or she grasps personally the truth of dying to the world. Paul, writing to the Galatians, said, "I have been crucified with Christ and I no longer live, but Christ lives in me. The life I now live in the body, I live by faith in the Son of God, who loved me and gave himself for me" (Galatians 2:20). For me, this rite of passage happened after a long period of restless debate about the purpose of life at work. In the early years, I was unclear that the work I was doing had any significance to God. I remember one day at lunchtime walking down the street that leads to the Bank of England. I saw ahead of me the fortress-like Bank of England, and to my left, the sign to the Swiss Bank Corporation (where I would later work). I remember looking at these signs—they projected great security. But then, in a flash, I saw the truth. No bank—Swiss Bank or Bank of England—would survive the promised return of Christ. Strong as they appeared, their apparent security would be broken in an instant. Decades later we see how even their argument of security has become an illusion.

I also realized in that moment the illusory nature of the idea of "job security."" True security can be found only in God's promises of security, both now and after death. I saw that Christ was in total control of all of life. Christ's death on the cross had broken the grip of this most forceful presence in my life: the desire for financial security for the future. I knew that I had died with Christ and now lived a new life in him. I could walk free from compulsive greed, false financial security, and captive illusions about the meaning of life. This did not mean that temptation ceased or that I never made wrong choices. But it did mean that the inevitability of being enthralled to the world was broken.

As Christians, in partnership with God, we each bring Christ's love to the world. But can love flourish in the workplace? After all, love and competition are not exactly twins. The idea is strained, not only because of the debased use of the word *love* to describe mere sexual encounters, but also because it is thought of as a "soft virtue," not one of the hard values that make for successful organizations. Surely the competitive drive of the business world forces love off the agenda. But, if love is central to the faith and if we are to be known by our love, how can it be excluded from the workplace? Love is the root motivation of service. Organizations frequently make the mistake of believing that good service to customers and clients can somehow be divorced from the internal attitudes of employees. But the opposite is the truth. When there are good internal attitudes, external service flourishes.

In *Joy at Work*, Dennis Bakke put it this way:

> It is love that allows us to treat each person in our organization
> with respect and dignity. Love sends people around the world

to serve others. Love inspires people to work with greater purpose. . . . Love makes it possible for me to forgive those who derided my views and caused me so much pain. Because love is directed toward others, it allows for the possibility that my critics were right and I was wrong. And if I was wrong, I would hope that love would enable my detractors to forgive the forceful way I pushed my philosophy.

I continue to believe that love is the final crucial ingredient in a joy-filled workplace. . . . Love is perfectly consistent with even the most aggressive economic goals.[3]

For me, love remains the key inheritance of faith and the missing jewel of happiness in the modern workplace. I hope this book will in a small way also help to recover the value and power of love at work.

The essence of the economy is a generosity of spirit: the desire to do well and to do good.

At the time of writing, my work involves running my own company to advise international clients on their strategic financial affairs. In my previous role as chairman of Lazard International investment bank, I was responsible for building relationships with key clients. I advised them on their strategies, helped them to buy and sell companies (including the high-profile sale of Harrods department store), and sometimes defended them from unwanted predators. I am also chairman of London Connection, founded by the bishop of London to reconnect business and ethics in the wake of the "Occupy" movement's protest outside St Paul's Cathedral in 2012. I was deeply struck by the passion of those demonstrators outside St Paul's Cathedral. At one level they could be seen as a ragtag mob, but at another, the ones with whom I engaged were as committed a group as I have ever met. Theirs was not a protest for its own sake but, rather, a compelling device to make the market economy more accountable and more transparent. It was an appropriate mission to have outside one of the United Kingdom's great cathedrals.

I recognize that my experience will be different from yours. However, in my conversation over the years with people working in very different jobs from mine, I have come to see that the underlying issues are similar for all Christians. Many people, at all stages of their working lives, have asked me questions about work and spirituality. I have been especially challenged by the questions of those in their twenties who are embarking on their careers, and those who are experiencing doubts about their role in the workplace. I have put pen to paper, I confess, reluctantly, as I do not find it easy to speak about myself. I can only hope that, from my own experience of hardship and joy in the workplace, you may catch some glimpse of God at work, and that he may help you as he has helped me. This book is for those who are already engaged in the exciting challenge of living out their Christian faith at work. It is also for those exploring the bigger questions of life who would describe themselves as sympathetic to Christianity, but not quite as shareholders who enjoy the risks and rewards of true ownership.

ONE

WORK MATTERS

IS GOD INTERESTED IN OUR WORK? MANY PEOPLE DO NOT SEE GOD as a 24/7 God, but as a withdrawn actor confined to a Sunday show with a declining audience. I have lost count of the number of times that I have heard people speak in such a way as to betray their belief that there is a divide between what is sacred and what is secular. Often, people portray church workers as being involved in sacred work, while I, as a banker, am seen to be involved in secular work. Nothing could be further from the truth: in God's eyes there is no such divide. It was Hudson Taylor who often declared, "Jesus Christ is either Lord of all, or he is not Lord at all."[1] Jesus is Lord over work in the financial world and in other sectors just as much as he is in the church world.

In the forty years I have lived in London, nothing has struck me so starkly as the false division of the sacred and the secular featured in the Millennium Dome (now known as the O_2 Arena) when it was built to commemorate the millennium. In this giant dome, a yearlong exhibition on life in the United Kingdom attempted to divide life into various spheres of activity, including a faith zone, a money zone, and a work zone. The clear message was that the faith zone was distinct from any other part of our lives. This distinction is a disastrous message. One cannot say that church is a "God zone" while the workplace is a "God-free zone." Christianity, in fact, involves our whole lives.

A key executive in a London trading firm once told me that his life at work had been completely transformed when he began to understand that God loved him as much in the frenzied atmosphere of the dealing room as he did at home or at church. Similarly, in the *Christian Herald*, artist Mark Cazalet said, "When I commit myself and my work into God's hands it means there is no split between the sacred and the secular, so everything I do becomes interconnected and part of my dialogue with God."[2] Operating with this integrated and interconnected worldview means that we need to live according to our Christian values in every area of our lives. I find it hugely challenging to ask myself each day at work how my own values have been influenced by the world and the degree to which they have shifted away from God toward myself.

So the world of work belongs not in the slipstream of twenty-first-century Christian spirituality, but in its mainstream. That's how God meant it to be. Yet, we will take our faith to work only if we know that our work is valuable to God.

GOD AT WORK

Mark Greene of the London Institute of Contemporary Christianity said, "Work is the primary activity God created us to pursue—in communion with him, and in partnership with others."[3] Right in the opening chapters of the Bible, we see three reasons why this is so, and why work matters so much to God.

As God was involved in the work of creation, he declared, "Let *us* make . . ." (Genesis 1:26, emphasis added), acknowledging that, in his very essence, he is relational. The Trinity is a perfect relationship between Father, Son, and Holy Spirit, working together in unity. God wants to share on earth what he sees working to perfection in the heavenly community of the Trinity. God has created for us the same attributes of sharing, service, partnership, collaboration, and interdependence that are the very essence of his character, and we see these attributes in work today.

The God of the Bible is not a passive, detached spiritual being but a dynamic, active, and entrepreneurial being. We see how God worked with extraordinary energy in creation to make the world, the animals, and, supremely, human life. He worked at full tilt to a timeline.

"WE WILL TAKE OUR FAITH TO WORK ONLY IF WE KNOW THAT OUR WORK IS VALUABLE TO GOD."

In Genesis 1, we read of his creative activities in making the heavens and the earth. After each day's work he had the supreme reward of reviewing each stage of his work and seeing that it was

3

good (v. 4). Moreover, life was not created as a one-off specification. He blessed the living creatures and commanded them to grow and to supply the earth and waters with increased production (v. 22). Although he felt good at each stage of the job, he did not stop until the task was completed to perfection (Genesis 2). Then he took time out and "rested from all the work of creating that he had done" (Genesis 2:3). He had worked with a purpose to establish creation. Thus, work was God's idea in the first place. Work matters to him.

In fact, God's work did not stop with the work of creation. All through the Bible, God is seen as a worker. He is described as a gardener (John 15:1), an artist (Genesis 1:1), a potter (Isaiah 64:8), a shepherd (John 10:11), a king (Psalm 145:1), a homemaker and a builder (Hebrews 3:4). Supremely, Jesus said, "My Father is always at his work to this very day, and I too am working" (John 5:17).

Just as Jesus' work on the earth reflected his Father, so each one of us is made in the image of God: "God created mankind in his own image, in the image of God he created them; male and female he created them" (Genesis 1:27). Therefore, just as God works, so each of us is made in order to work too. As God labored in creation, so we are to do the same.

Of course, Jesus is the perfect image of God, untainted by sin. Paul wrote that Jesus "is the image of the invisible God. . . . He is before all things, and in him all things hold together" (Colossians 1:15–17), and Jesus, this perfect image, worked. As a young man, Jesus, like many of his contemporaries, would have worked in the family business with his earthly father, Joseph, learning

skills both in manufac-
turing and in dealing
with people. We can
easily imagine Jesus pur-
chasing wood and nails,
making a window or
door, negotiating a price,
and selling his work. In
these hidden years, Jesus
must have come into
contact with a cross-

> "HE DID NOT COME TO GIVE US A NEW FORM OF SPIRITUAL LIFE DISCONNECTED FROM THE WORLD. HE CAME TO CONTINUE AND RESTORE THE PATTERNS OF WORK AND SERVICE INITIATED BY HIS FATHER."

section of the community in Nazareth. This is reflected in his
teaching, which includes references to workers in the vineyard,
meetings with tax collectors, dealings with agents, and discussions about money, livestock, and property. He did not come to
give us a new form of spiritual life disconnected from the world.
He came to continue and restore the patterns of work and service initiated by his Father. We need to look to do the same. The
importance of work does not just come indirectly from the fact
that God works and we are made in his image. It also comes
directly. God, in fact, *commands* us to work.

God has given us a creation mandate to be stewards of the
created order (Genesis 1:28). Eugene Peterson's *The Message* translation of the Bible includes terms such as "prosper," "take charge,"
and "be responsible" in this passage. God wants us to establish a
community on earth based on mutual service. Just as God serves,
so he commands us to serve through our work: "the LORD God
took the man and put him in the Garden of Eden to work it and

take care of it" (Genesis 2:15). Furthermore, Adam and Eve experienced fulfillment as human beings as they served God in their work, which was as closely allied to God's purposes as it was possible to be. Work was in the original God-breathed prospectus.

However, Adam and Eve were drawn away from God as they disobeyed his command not to eat the fruit from the tree of the knowledge of good and evil. After the fall they had to make the harsh adjustment to encumbered work. Futility, despair, recrimination, broken relationships, and, ultimately, death entered the world and the workplace as a result. Work became difficult "toil" (Genesis 3:17–19); the whole created order broke away from its cooperation with God, which meant that the ground was cursed and work became "painful"—a living had to be earned by the sweat of our brows. Almost everything was different from that point on, yet God's mandate to work remained the same: "So the LORD God banished him from the Garden of Eden to work the ground from which he had been taken" (Genesis 3:23).

But everything within the Creator wanted to restore work to its original specification. A new initiative was needed to enable the broken model to work again. And so it was that Jesus was sent with a mandate to repair the fractured working relationship between us and God. He came to pay off the debt that bound work to futility.

WORK—FULFILLMENT OR FUTILITY?

A new trainee once told me, as we were discussing our work: "Let's face it. We work to make money, to live, and to enjoy ourselves. It makes life bearable even if work sucks. What's so wrong with that?" The truth is that work now exists in a tension between fulfillment and futility. On the one hand we know the presence of God at work, creating, innovating, and filling us with energy. We see signs of his activity in the many ways in which we flourish at work and feel good about our achievements. On the other hand we know the futility of work, the lack of direction, the struggle to get things done, and the frustration of difficult colleagues, stressful situations, and plans not working out as we had hoped.

No one who was working in London in October 2008 will forget that crucial Friday when it appeared that RBS (the Royal Bank of Scotland), one of the world's largest banks, would collapse. Alistair Darling, then Chancellor of the Exchequer, was rumored to have asked Tom McKillop, the then Chairman of RBS, "How long can you hold out?" The reply was chilling: "Two or three hours." I remember sitting at my desk in the West End of London with a number of senior colleagues. We all knew the consequences of RBS failing: every ATM would seize up; there would be no cash in the system; and money in transit would not be honored. Someone buying a house would not have the deposit cleared—the purchaser would be in default. The situation was horrendous. I remember the icy nature of fear and the futility felt by all; there was very little that could be done.

We immediately set to work to gather our thoughts and try to provide advice to some of the major banks and clients we were advising at the time. However, the sense of powerlessness in the face of a failing banking system was pervasive. Nonetheless I realized that out of this crisis there were a number of opportunities: to think clearly and to provide good advice, even though the future (as is always the case) was unclear and particularly uncertain.

I knew that the future belonged to God alone and, for whatever reason, he had allowed a massive shake-up of the financial system in the world. Our task was, therefore, to read the signs and as best possible to be prepared to deal with future uncertainty. This became the most intellectually stimulating, but deeply frustrating and challenging part of my career thus far. This is often the case when we look at the workplace—we see apparent futility when we can't see the overall purpose. Fulfillment comes from finding meaning and purpose in our actual day-to-day work, without necessarily knowing that the whole system or individual transaction is going to be a success. Futility and frustration are twins.

But, we live with hope for the future. Because work was part of God's original plan for humanity, we know that he will maintain the best of the original creation when he calls into being the new heaven and the new earth (Revelation 21:24, 26). Eternity will involve perfect work—the work of serving the Lord Jesus Christ (Revelation 22:3).

It is work that utterly fulfills and which is in no way futile. As was God's original purpose, it is perfect service rather than imperfect servitude. But to make the most of our lives on earth we need to have a clear view of God's intentions for us in the workplace: to serve him and our community and to enjoy a measure of success, to grow in our humanity, and to influence the world for good as we wait for Jesus to return. This is not merely a case of chalking up air miles while we are alive to be spent in heaven after death. Eternal life starts here as we live well for God, reflecting his original intentions by participating in turning around the broken image of work.

Work will never be perfected until the return of Jesus but, until then, it is possible, as I have found in my over-forty-year career, through the power of his Spirit, to live and work together with purpose, direction, and enjoyment.

HOLY JOBS—BISHOPS AND BANKERS

In *A Parable of the Wicked Mammon* (1528), William Tyndale, the translator of the Bible into English, said:

> There is no work better than another to please God; to pour
> water, to wash dishes, to be a souter [cobbler], or an apostle,
> all is one; to wash dishes and to preach is all one, as touching
> the deed, to please God.[4]

We need not only to recover this understanding, but also to rid ourselves of the view that there is a religious pecking order in God's sight where bishops rank ahead of bankers and ordained clergy ahead of computer programmers. Throughout the centuries this division has, unfortunately, still continued. The distinction is deep rooted, going back to the medieval exaltation of the clergy and continuing to the time when the links between

God and ordinary daily life were severed in the name of progress and reason. Clericalism had let the educated clerical class be the sole exponents of Christianity, disenfranchising everyone else. But the New Testament writer Paul drew no distinction between hard spiritual work and hard work in the workplace. He used the same words to discuss manual labor as he did apostolic service.

The reality is that all jobs are equal. Throughout Scripture we find God's people involved in a vast array of different jobs: Abraham was a cattle trader; Joseph was prime minister and later dabbled in wheat futures; Luke was a doctor; the first Ethiopian convert was a central banker; Dorcas was in fashion; Simon the tanner was the Louis Vuitton of his day; and Jesus was, of course, a carpenter. For me, this realization transformed the way in which I viewed the workplace. God was interested in every aspect of my life. At church on Sunday, we may pray for the leaders of the church and society, but how often do we pray for Sarah the accountant and Mark the salesman in the third row?

Christians have, at times, adopted the great fallacy that an emigration from the world of work would produce a spirituality of a higher order that would, therefore, be more pleasing to God. The monastic tradition, often blamed for this withdrawal from the world, has, on the contrary, a high view of work. We cannot, and were never intended by God to, take exit visas from the world to escape its pressures. Theologian Dietrich Bonhoeffer, in *Letters and Papers from Prison*, spoke of the calling of Christians to be "this worldly," living amongst the harsh realities of life and demonstrating our faith by the day-to-day choices we make.[5] Before Jesus was arrested, he prayed for his disciples: "My prayer is not that you take them out of the world but that you protect them from the evil one" (John 17:15). We have been created by God to work in this world.

MY WORK STATION IS MY WORSHIP STATION

I've never been able to see how this computer has anything to do with the kingdom of God.

—JIM BANKS, COMPUTER PROGRAMMER

So, why do we work? Is it really a necessary evil? There are many reasons for working:

- Professional—to fulfill career objectives
- Achievement—to reach a life goal
- Economic—to create wealth
- Financial—to support oneself and a family
- Personal—to experience fulfillment and significance
- Social—to avoid being a burden on others
- Relational—to support other people through collaborative effort

Yet, perhaps the ultimate overarching purpose for work is to worship God in and through our work. Famously, the first question in the Westminster Catechism written in the 1640s is "What is the chief and highest end of man?" and the answer given is that "Man's chief and highest end is to glorify God, and fully to enjoy him forever." We can glorify God and enjoy him in and through our work. Our work is a form of worship to God.

So, when I am asked about worship, I reply firmly, "My work station is my worship station." Worship is the total submission of our whole person to the glory of God as we recognize our dependence on him. My desk should therefore be a place of worship. Indeed, there is a Hebrew word—*avad*—that can mean either to work or to worship. God is our real employer. In his letter to the Colossians, Paul urges us, "Whatever you do, work at it with all your heart, as working for the Lord, not for human masters" (Colossians 3:23). I remember a personal assistant telling me that, when she passed the reception desk on her way into work each morning, she reminded herself, "It is the Lord Christ I serve." This avoids the danger of settling for satisfactory underperformance. I try to pray every morning as I start work because I want to remind myself that I am not dependent on myself or on any economic system, but on God. Work is a ministry, empowered by God, for the benefit of ourselves and others and, ultimately, for his glory.

When Jesus came to earth, he proclaimed that the kingdom of God was at hand. The language of kingdoms can sound strange to us, in that it seems to signify territoriality. In the context of work, it may therefore be helpful to see the kingdom of God as "the sphere of God's goodness" in the world. We are called to advance God's kingdom, sharing the "sphere of goodness" and extending it as we operate with God's values. Our actions at work have the potential to advance the kingdom of

God and his "sphere of goodness," or to hinder it—on both a macro and a micro level. Each time we tell the truth, make decisions fairly and with respect for others, or act with integrity, we are advancing this sphere, albeit in small ways.

PROFIT OR NOT?

I am often asked the question whether it would not be better to work for a charity or for a church than in the business world. I understand the question, but the answer is not obvious and relies on the mistaken belief that God is more interested in the apparently greater humanitarian activities of a charity than he is in more typical work.

He isn't. He wants us to know how much he values

> "WE ARE CALLED TO ADVANCE GOD'S KINGDOM, SHARING THE 'SPHERE OF GOODNESS' ... AS WE OPERATE WITH GOD'S VALUES."

our workplaces, so that we are free to work without guilt. Some, of course, will be called to work in the voluntary sector. However, most of us will find our callings in a for-profit organization and will need to find out the purpose for us in doing our jobs. In practice, it is easier to see this in some jobs, such as nursing or social work, than in others. You can work in a not-for-profit organization, but you cannot work in a not-for-purpose organization.

> "YOU CAN WORK IN A NOT-FOR-PROFIT ORGANIZATION, BUT YOU CANNOT WORK IN A NOT-FOR-PURPOSE ORGANIZATION."

How then does working in a large organization advance the kingdom of God? An executive five years into a career at a major supermarket chain said:

I spent the first three years of my career wondering what the point of my work was—I was such a small cog in a huge wheel. I felt completely insignificant; that I could never make a difference. I then went through the God at Work course with a group of people at church and a lightbulb went on in my head—I now knew that my day-to-day work mattered to God and was of ultimate importance. I have never looked back.

—TIM RICHARDS

Understanding the bigger picture is an essential requirement if we are to find the purpose behind our work.

At the macro level, the free flow of capital, the provision of funds for new business, and the creation of jobs are all important to society. We all need to understand the wider context of the jobs we do. For example, the supermarket manager delivers a crucial service by providing good food at affordable prices. Effective management and customer service impacts the community by making shopping a positive experience.

At the micro level, as we learn to see what God is doing in

our workplaces, we can then put our energies into those areas. For example, whether we describe a product accurately or not is a spiritual decision. When we declare truth even in small measures, the kingdom of God is advanced. This can be true when we draft documents, design packaging, give business advice, sell products, create websites, or mark exams—indeed, in any activity we do in our working day.

We need to remind ourselves continuously that God is interested in building up his original plan of community. We often miss out on this crucial reason for work by narrowing the discussion on the purpose of work to an individualistic debate about self-fulfillment. Instead, this debate should be held in the context of the needs of the wider human community that God created, loves, and intended for banks, supermarkets, hospitals, information technology, and other businesses to serve.

FRUITFUL AND FAITHFUL—HOW DO WE MAKE A DIFFERENCE?

Most people want to make a difference with their lives. To do this, we have to identify our part in extending God's kingdom. The great task of the Christian in the world today is to bring blessing to the world. We are agents for good living in the world as we encourage people to connect with God and with each other. Of course, we will all have different levels of influence. Someone at the bottom rung of the ladder of their job may just be able to influence the lives of the few colleagues they work with, whereas the chief executive will be able to influence lots of individuals, as well as the whole structure and strategy of the company. Nonetheless, in whatever role we find ourselves, we need to be both fruitful and faithful in pursuing our God-given ambitions. In the parable of the talents (Matthew 25:14–30; Luke 19:11–27), the master, before going on a journey to have himself appointed king, gives his servants some capital and urges them to put it to work until he returns. When he returns, he rewards the two servants who have put the money to good use and have made more from the initial gift, associating themselves with him in his absence, despite his general lack of popularity. However, he is angry with the servant who merely preserved the initial capital without taking the necessary risks to make it grow.

We need to be faithful to God, willing to associate ourselves with his values in the workplace. This may risk our reputations because, as Christians, we have to face the taunt that there is no God, or else, if there is one, as in the parable, he appears to have gone on a long holiday. We, however, behave each day in the knowledge that Jesus will return and reward us, as well as call us to account.

I remember being on holiday in the south of France and seeing a magnificent yacht moored in harbor. I met the captain, who was having coffee in the marina, and asked him about the yacht. He told me that every day the crew of twenty-four took her out to sea to check on safety procedures. Every day the yacht was cleaned to perfection. She was provisioned, and every day they were ready to sail. He then added, wistfully, "We have not seen or heard from the owner for nearly three years, but we are ready to set sail the moment he arrives, and I know he will turn up one day, I hope soon." This is how we should live, getting on with the job in hand, as well as we can, as we anticipate the return of Jesus.

We are to be fruitful as well as faithful. We need growth in all areas of life—there is no steady state. Our talents, money, time, and resources are all God's gift to us and should be used well. Making the most of them will involve risk. The key point of this parable is that the hand of fruitfulness needs the glove of faithfulness in order to grasp the opportunities that we are given. We cannot merely be faithful, simply taking what God has given us, preserving it, pickling it, and then producing it upon his return. Equally, we cannot merely be fruitful, simply adding to the resources he has given, without recognizing at the same time that we are servants awaiting the return of our master. As Paul instructs us all, the purpose of our work and our lives is to "make the most of every opportunity" (Colossians 4:5).

> "OUR TALENTS, MONEY, TIME, AND RESOURCES ARE ALL GOD'S GIFT TO US AND SHOULD BE USED WELL. MAKING THE MOST OF THEM WILL INVOLVE RISK."

TWO

WORK AND THE WORLD

THE WORLD—TO COMFORT OR CONFRONT?

God loves the world. This is evident throughout Scripture and is given full expression in John 3:16: "For God so loved the world that he gave his one and only Son, that whoever believes in him shall not perish but have eternal life." Yet John also warned us: "Do not love the world or anything in the world" (1 John 2:15). The apparent contradiction in these verses is easily resolved. We are not to "love the world," meaning that part of creation that seeks to run itself without any reference to God. This world-view is articulated, for example, through the media, which often reflects opinions made by people for people, but without the acknowledgment of God. The theologian Walter Brueggemann calls this absence of God "the defining pathology of our time."[1] The world in this wrong-headed sense cannot recognize the hand of God; and because it is on a trajectory to destruction, we are not to set our hearts on it. However, we are to love the world that God has created: the environment (which he has given to us to preserve for future generations) and people, whom God created and for whom Christ died.

Our workplaces are structured organizations. In the course of a career, many of us will both be managed and manage others and most of us will have peer colleagues. These distinctions affect both the information that it is appropriate to share and our method of communication. However, we need to remember that people are still people. Behind the suits and uniforms live vulnerable individuals in need of affirmation and support. We all need commendation and recognition for the positive things we do at work. Day to day we need to seek opportunities to go against the grain: to offer small acts of kindness or words of encouragement to our colleagues, or simply to be positive in negative situations. I know a lawyer who makes a point of complimenting at least one person in the office each day. His aim is to counter the negative words spoken around him. Learning to love our neighbor, surely the hallmark of the Christian faith, is tested each day in the fire of the workplace.

SO HOW DO WE SHOW GOD'S LOVE AT WORK?

In 1995, SG Warburg, the London-based investment bank for which I was working, was subject to a takeover bid by the Swiss Bank Corporation. As anyone knows, changing jobs is in itself a difficult and uncertain process. It becomes more so when the institution as a whole is taken over. It is not a pleasant feeling: there are an enormous number of uncertainties and the future is unknown. Promises are often made without the expectation that they will be fulfilled, and a deeply cynical and negative culture takes hold.

Senior managers at SG Warburg had to make decisions on who would be retained and who would be sacked. A pool of funds was made available to the bank by Swiss Bank Corporation to use as a retention payment for the employees. The question was, how would this money be divided? Would the best employees receive most, or would it be spread widely? The prevailing view in similar situations was to give most to the best and to leave others with little or no payment. I thought, however, at a time of uncertainty and fearfulness, that it was right that the benefits should be spread more widely than would be customary. I was delighted that the senior colleagues were of a similar view. The workplace provides opportunities to go against the grain. We may not always be supported as I was in this case, but taking a different view challenges the status quo and is part of Jesus' mandate to love our neighbor as ourselves.

In John 17, Jesus outlined an inherent tension, saying that his followers are in the world but not of the world. By this, he meant that, although we aim to operate by the values of the kingdom of God, geographically we are located in the workplaces of the world. As we walk through the fields of life, we pick up burrs of loneliness, disappointment, and purposelessness. We find ourselves both bearing and breaking the image of a dysfunctional society. This is the daily confrontation in the workplace and this tension leads to a constant negotiation of complex issues for which there are no pre-agreed outcomes. In one sense, the workplace is a battleground, but the victory is assured. I constantly remind myself that "no weapon that is formed against [me] shall prosper" (Isaiah 54:17 KJV). We still have to live with uncertainty and complexity, but we have not been left without assistance: the Holy Spirit comes alongside to help us.

How, then, do we make the most of living in the world? Many Christians have a way of looking at the world with an ingrained pessimism. Preachers, wishing to draw distinctions, can also fall into this habit of describing the world in lurid terms in order to accentuate the theme of the great escape to salvation. The willingness to criticize the world and its aspirations at every opportunity has caused an imbalance in our attitude toward it. How do we correct this perspective, while remaining alive to the seductive nature of the world and its aspirations? I have found three approaches to be helpful.

1. Understanding the world

Jesus wanted people to understand reality. We need to learn from him and to sharpen our analytical tools when trying to understand the world before we launch into a critical tirade against its defects. Our first rule of engagement with the world is, therefore, to try to understand its aspirations and desires and to embrace its goodness. I was struck by reading the parable of the unjust steward in Luke 16:1–8, where Jesus made what appears to be a cryptic conclusion. He said that the "people of this world" are often shrewder in dealing with the issues facing them in the world than the people of light (meaning those of faith). Jesus seemed to be suggesting that the world understands itself better than outsiders do. When we listen to contemporary music, watch films, or study advertising messages, we soon discover this to be true.

The question of whether the world is an enlightened or a dark place is a crucial one for anyone attempting to live for Christ in the workplace. We need a biblical worldview if we are to live meaningful lives in the world. One only has to look at the successful advertising of the technology company Apple over the last thirty years to see the desire for purpose, belonging, motivation, and identity that exists in the world. The company's slogans "Think Differently," "Life made easier," "Play more than music. Play a part" (for a 2006 iPod campaign), and "Share the fun," all speak of belonging and the power of community, united by a product. These slogans were created as one of the world's leading companies tried to understand and connect with the perceived needs of people, indeed even creating "whole new devices and services that customers did not yet know they needed."[2] We thus learn from the media, songwriters, advertisers, and opinion-formers about the needs of the world. Our understanding is improved when we become involved in discussion and dialogue with those who do not share Christian assumptions of life. By understanding where they are, we can begin to help shift the basis of their worldview away from the fruitless search for meaning, "chasing after the wind" (Ecclesiastes 1:14), or the deficient solutions offered by the world.

2. Critiquing the world

It is, however, not sufficient merely to understand and to show empathy toward the world around us. Nor should we be gullible and allow the world to define its own solutions. There is a need for a rational and critical review of the defects of the world in which we live. The prevailing values of the world should be held to account to test whether these values are serving the interests of society or destroying them. The 2008–09 global financial crisis provided a catalyst for urgent examination of these values. So, for example, we assess the driving forces behind consumerism to determine how they are at odds with the biblical values of restraint and generosity to others. Among the many casually held assumptions the financial crisis swept away was the dangerous idea that business, not just finance, can be conducted without being grounded in considerations other than the purely financial. The crisis reinforced in my mind a conviction that had been forming for some time: economic and social progress depends on reintegrating the three-legged stool of the moral, spiritual, and financial dimensions of our lives. It depends on having the strength to assert what is right and reject what is wrong. It depends on saying that there are such things as right and wrong and, therefore, on understanding in the fullest sense, what it means to be human.

Distinguishing right from wrong confronts head-on the prevailing consensus that you can atomize a person; that public values and private values need not meet. The consequences of this conviction reach into all aspects of life, not just business. The UK parliamentary expenses scandal grew out of thinking that mere adherence to the rules conferred legitimacy. Like the financial crisis, the scandal would never have occurred had professed public virtues and private virtues been the same. There is no separation between a private life and a public life: both influence the other. Together they establish character and the nature of our humanity.

The world cannot simply turn this thinking on its head, nor can it produce solutions for unhappiness or lack of fulfillment at work, for fractured relationships or depression and stress—it has no answer for the world's conundrums: how, for example, to marry the desire for instant gratification with the long-term formation of character. A biblical critique is part of the process of establishing the vacuum that exists in the world's perceptions.

3. Drawing the world to Christ

After understanding the world and critiquing its failures, the third and distinctive engagement takes place. We are to be witnesses to the power of God's activity in reconciling the world to himself. The way ahead lies not merely in understanding more clearly the wider needs of our colleagues, nor in the skill with which these needs are examined and commented upon. Real change comes from being able to introduce Christ's teaching and power into the dialogue with the world. I do not see this in adversarial terms but as part of a dialectic that starts with understanding, before it becomes prescriptive. The cross is the central tenet of the Christian faith and the lens through which we see the world. In contrast, many have tried to seek reconciliation with the world through a myriad of spiritual doctrines and experiences, all of which duck the central Christian event—the cross—in the hope of finding the power to live a cross-less spiritual experience. Such a route is doomed to fail. It is through the cross and resurrection that reconciliation with the world takes place. There are no shortcuts, and our challenge is to present this insight in everyday language to a world searching for its anchor.

Let us apply these three critical tools—understanding the world, critiquing the world, and drawing the world to Christ—to the current debate on the search for happiness. While the pursuit of happiness is not a modern invention, there seems to be a new intensity about the contemporary quest for happiness. The UK prime minister David Cameron urged us to remember "what makes people happy, as well as what makes stock markets rise . . . it is time to be focused not just on GDP but on GWB—General Well Being."[3] To this end, Cameron's government introduced the National Well-Being Survey in 2011. A leading article in the *Sunday Times* described the quest for happiness as follows:

> It has become the great obsession, spawning dozens of books and growing a number of university and school courses, here and in America. Happiness is in vogue.[4]

What was previously left to philosophers is now the object of study by economists, social scientists, and business schools. There is even an increasing number of Christian books on how to find happiness. The John Lewis Partnership, one of the United Kingdom's most successful retailers, states unambiguously that "the Partnership's ultimate purpose is the happiness of all its members through their worthwhile and satisfying employment in a successful business."[5] Happiness is important to us all, whether viewed from a faith base or not. The Dalai Lama's book *The Art of Happiness: A Handbook for Living* is an international bestseller. William James, the American philosopher, spoke of happiness as the real motivation of all people: "How to gain, how to keep, how to recover happiness, is in fact for most men at all times the secret motive of all they do, and of all they are willing to endure."[6]

The questions, however, leap out at once: Why do we have so much and are still unhappy? What is happiness? Where does it come from? Can it be taken in tablet form? Do we merely resign ourselves to Immanuel Kant's comment, "the notion of happiness is so indeterminate that although every human being wishes to attain it, yet he never can say definitely and consistently what it is that he really wishes and wills"?[7]

We understand the world's longing for happiness but also see the deficiency of its tools in trying to understand the nature of true happiness. But, even in terms of prevailing values without a distinctively Christian interpretation, there is a recognition that this longing to be happy at work and in life generally is important and not merely a current fad.

Happiness will not be found in possessions, more spending, greater material prosperity, or greater job satisfaction. Oliver James's book *Affluenza*, a *Sunday Times* bestseller, speaks of the "virus" of consumerism that is sweeping the western world. The psychologist's research shows that the desire and pursuit of material wealth has left us twice as prone to depression, anxiety, and addictions than the non-Western world.[8] The Legatum Institute's Global Prosperity Index,[9] which analyzes prosperity in more than one hundred countries (by measuring access to health care, GDP, respect for human rights, unemployment, and working hours, among other criteria), has found that, once beyond the poverty level, individuals' happiness does not increase with a proliferation in personal wealth. Happiness and purposeful living go together. When asked what it was like to be the wealthiest person in the world, Bill Gates replied that he wished he were not the richest man.[10] But I don't know anyone who would not want to be the happiest person in the world. On a smaller scale, we need to ask the question of whether our daily working lives are so focused on earning and advancement that we have neglected to find the source of sustainable happiness.

When we draw these desires together we realize that merely being happy for a day because a project has been successfully completed is not enough. To be truly happy requires something greater than the satisfaction of my own interests. Helping others, being generous with time as well as with money, and being prepared to put the interests of others before those of one's self show the altruism inherent in the search for happiness.

> "ARE OUR DAILY WORKING LIVES SO FOCUSED ON EARNING AND ADVANCEMENT THAT WE NEGLECT FINDING THE SOURCE OF SUSTAINABLE HAPPINESS?"

What, then, does Christian spirituality have to offer a

generation longing for consistent day-in and day-out happiness in the workplace? Here we hit the reality block. Christian values, based on the teachings of Jesus, are often countercultural. It is simply not possible to live in a cocooned world, expecting to be happy every moment. To believe this would be to live in a fool's paradise. Jesus said that in this world we "will have trouble." But, as ever, while recognizing the reality of living in a world adrift from its Creator's moorings, Jesus went on to promise: "But take heart! I have overcome the world" (John 16:33). There will, therefore, be times of sorrow, mourning, difficulties, and unhappiness. There will also be days when, if we are honest, we feel neither one way nor the other—and life goes on. What we need to do, therefore, is to enter a dialogue of reality with those searching for happiness and base this interchange upon the teachings of Christ. Happiness is therefore redefined not just as an unlinked series of fleeting feelings of enjoyment but as a part of the overall search for purpose in life. The closer we live in line with the wisdom of Christ's teachings, the more we will be able to accept the joy of moments of happiness while also being able to live with the down times. The truth is that our search for happiness will be most fulfilled when seen through the lens of Christ's teaching on sacrifice, service, contentment, and joy. When we allow the interests of others to flourish at work at our expense, we may well feel tugs of unhappiness but, in the overall scheme of living for Christ, these acts of self-denial become a pattern of lasting joy, which St Paul summed up when he said, "For to me, to live is Christ" (Philippians 1:21). True joy, happiness, and fulfillment run together when the focus moves from ourselves to helping satisfy the needs and aspirations of others. So, the Living Bible translation rightly paraphrases the "Blessed are those" sayings in the Sermon on the Mount as, "Happy are those . . ."; "Happy are those who long to be just and good, for they shall be completely satisfied" (Matthew 5:6). They may know times of unhappiness, but they are happy overall because they have been satisfied by knowing that they are living by the original plan of God's intentions to all people on earth.

In this way, we understand the world's longing for happiness and recognize that even by its own standards happiness will not be obtained through the pursuit of materialist solutions. Instead, we need to point to the cross and resurrection in order to reinterpret happiness: when understood in this light, this makes sense of the pursuit of happiness. An image that I find helpful is that of the television screen. If you turn on a news channel or business channel, not only do you see the images of current world events unfolding, but below the pictures there is often a running text giving additional information and "breaking news." I see this as an illustration of the Christian's interaction with the world. As we see and hear world events breaking, we should constantly be running a biblical commentary on these

> "THE TRUTH IS THAT OUR SEARCH FOR HAPPINESS WILL BE MOST FULFILLED WHEN SEEN THROUGH THE LENS OF CHRIST'S TEACHING ON SACRIFICE, SERVICE, CONTENTMENT, AND JOY."

events, interpreting actions, and reminding ourselves that we only truly come to understand the world in and through Christ.

Too often, the church has tried to urge people to live by the values of Christ without paying sufficient attention to the pressures of day-to-day life, appearing self-righteous in its judgments as well as being insensitive and escapist. As we engage with society's issues, we are called to confront anything that draws people away from God, but at the same time to comfort those who are struggling. But how often does our society end up confronting those who need comforting and comforting those who need confronting?

During the global Occupy movement in 2012, protestors camped on the steps of St Paul's Cathedral in London for weeks on end. Following the resignation of the dean and the canon chancellor of the cathedral, the bishop of London asked me to become involved in the dialogue and negotiation with the demonstrators, appointing me chair of London Connection, which seeks to reconnect the financial with the ethical. It was an extremely stimulating assignment. The demonstrators were a mixture of supporters of every kind of cause imaginable, but I was struck by a core of young people who were seriously concerned about the market economy. Thankfully, the protests ended peacefully.

We made a commitment to the protestors that we would seek a continuing dialogue in order to ensure that the ethical issues that they raised were addressed by those in authority in the city and in our major financial institutions. One particularly memorable meeting brought together Hector Sants, then chair of the Financial Services Authority, the bishop of London, and a group of protestors. We met in a tent in the grounds of St Ethelburga's church. While squatting shoeless on the floor, I feared the worst, expecting as much ranting and shouting as had been broadcast daily on our TV screens. Yet the meeting was extraordinary for the perceptiveness of the questioning and the deep unease expressed by those who felt let down by the system. The question they posed was profound: If capitalism is so good for us all, then why is it not delivering for young people? This is an almost unanswerable question. It had a profound effect on me.

I realized then that we need to redouble our efforts to engage with young people who are entering the workplace, to enable them to refashion the market economy into a more responsible, values-driven community. What also struck me was the importance the demonstrators clearly put on the creation of wealth. They weren't unhinged Marxists, but had a deep spiritual commitment to finding a solution to a human problem. A new generation is growing up whose values are very different from those of the people who caused the near cardiac arrest of the financial system. I realized that a return to our Christian roots as the basis for finding a moral system that will infuse the market economy is an objective worth working toward.

The global financial crisis brought about a new normal: it cannot be business as usual anymore. I remain committed to the view, shared by many young people in multiple conversations on the steps of St Paul's Cathedral, that the creation of wealth is a moral imperative of our time, but it cannot be an absolute.

It needs to be seen in the context of the re-humanizing of our financial and business community. If I ever needed persuasion that the essence of the Christian message is for people at work, it is this—that the Spirit of God makes us not more religious, but more human.

Sometimes the harsh working environment seems the last place I would expect to meet God. However, Jesus experienced the worst of the world on the cross. My office may seem very far from the goodness of God, but, in fact, he has gone a lot further. The cross is the furthest place of human despair. He went there for us. However godless a workplace may appear, it is not beyond his reach. It is not a no-God area. Jesus' resurrection is the constant reminder of life beyond the struggle. In hard times, when the world seems to close in on us or we become self-obsessed, I have found that repeating aloud the simple truth that "Christ is risen" has a transforming power. This is the pointer to life in all its fullness. The reminder that tomorrow will come is the assurance we all need to enable us to live in hope each day. This knowledge provides daily reassurance as we face a tough workplace.

> "IN HARD TIMES, WHEN THE WORLD SEEMS TO CLOSE IN ON US OR WE BECOME SELF-OBSESSED, I HAVE FOUND THAT REPEATING ALOUD THE SIMPLE TRUTH THAT 'CHRIST IS RISEN' HAS A TRANSFORMING POWER."

People matter to God and, therefore, to us. An important

aspect of loving those we work with is to pray for them, mostly without their knowing. We may be aware that there are people in our workplace with questions about the meaning of life and the existence of God, who would value our input as part of their search. We need to be ready to answer, when asked about our faith, clearly and without embarrassment. But our prime task at work is not to be evangelists. That is not what we are employed to do. However, we should be vigilant and available to colleagues at decisive moments when we can discuss with them the way toward a spirituality that will enrich their lives.

The thoughts of this chapter can best be summed up in the story of a friend of mine:

I was brought up in a Christian family in New Zealand, with my great-grandfather being a Methodist missionary. When I was ten years old my younger sister died and my parents were divorced soon after. Our family then drifted away from our faith. When I graduated, I chose a career in banking and found myself working at Warburg's in London in the early 1990s. I was achieving the career and financial objectives I'd set myself; I'd married a beautiful American woman; we spent our weekends in romantic European cities—what more could I want? I found myself feeling strangely empty, but resolutely dismissed the emotion as "Sunday night blues." But increasingly I wondered, "Is there more to life than this?"

I was working for a man named Ken Costa and found myself regularly traveling in taxis with him to and from meetings. The traffic in London is terrible, so there was a lot of time to talk! Ken found out somehow about the scrap of Christianity in my life and invited me to an Alpha Party [to introduce the Alpha Course]. When my wife, Katie, questioned me on the invitation, I told her that the guy was my boss and we had to go! The truth was, though, that I had come to respect him and was curious about his views. We duly turned up and Nicky Gumbel [vicar of HTB] gave a talk. The talk was excellent but what interested me were the people who stood up and said that God was filling an emptiness inside them, the very emotion with which I wrestled.

To be honest, Ken played no further part in my search for God. He never mentioned Alpha again. He had effectively stepped aside to let God do the work. At the Alpha Weekend, I became a Christian, and subsequently engineered lunch with Ken to ask him a burning question: Must I give all this up and become a missionary to India? I dreaded the answer. But Ken assured me that God does not lead us out of jobs, but into them, and I stayed in investment banking.

Soon after, Katie and I moved to Australia and became involved in Alpha at our local church in Melbourne. In 1998, whilst still working full-time in investment banking, I became chairman of Alpha Australia. In 2000, I joined the board of Alpha International. At the beginning of 2004, while walking along a beach in Sydney, Nicky Gumbel asked me to become chairman of Alpha Asia Pacific. Finally, I was called out of investment banking as God gave me a passion to fulfill all the skills honed over twenty years in banking, but now of course I am doing deals for God!

In 1991, I was terrified of becoming a missionary to India. In March 2005, in a meeting in Mumbai, I suddenly realized I had become a missionary to India. And now I find myself sitting on the Alpha International Board with Ken Costa, and even occasionally sharing a taxi!

THREE

AMBITION AND LIFE CHOICES

THE WORD *AMBITION* ELICITS A MIXED RESPONSE. FOR THE ACTOR
Johnny Depp, "Ambition has become a dirty word."[1] So too the
band Radiohead: "Ambition makes you look pretty ugly."[2] But
it's not all negative. When we hear of athletes wanting to win a
gold medal, we applaud their single-minded ambition.

Many Christians regard ambition for anything other than
"saving souls" as a distraction from what they regard as our true
calling to evangelism. This is a misunderstanding of the Bible:
God has called us to extend his kingdom in the world in partnership with him. This can apply to many aspects of life, not
just so-called Christian work. It is surely right to be ambitious
about our contribution to this. Christians sometimes feel that
it is inappropriate to pray for opportunity and success at work.
Yet, in 1 Chronicles 4:9–10, Jabez, a man described as "more
honorable than his brothers," prayed that God would bless him

and increase his possessions. If our ambition is aligned with what God has called us to do, then we are right to ask for his blessing on it so that we can make a difference in the world and bring him glory.

Sir Rocco Forte, who lost a hotel chain built up by his father and went on to build a chain of his own, summed up the desires of many when he reflected, "I don't want to go through life and for people to say 'What have you done?' and to say 'Nothing.' I like to feel that I've made an impact, left something behind."[3]

PASSIONATE AND CONTENTED— WHAT IS CHRISTIAN AMBITION?

For me, Christian ambition is the passionate and contented pursuit of challenging, yet attainable, God-given objectives.

Passionate

In *Blood and Fire*, the biography of General William Booth, politician Roy Hattersley described the "reckless enthusiasm" that led Booth to form the Salvation Army in 1865.[4] Similarly, our ambitions should arise from a God-given passion: to fulfill his purpose for our lives. In Philippians, Paul wrote, "It is God who works in you *to will* and to act according to his good purpose" (2:13, emphasis added).

Jean-Pierre Garnier, the former head of GlaxoSmithKline, one of the world's largest pharmaceutical companies, put it succinctly: "I don't know anyone who is passionate and unsuccessful."[5]

Contented

God gives us objectives that match our talents. Romans 12:6 is clear: "We have different gifts." If you are unsure of what your talents are, it may be worth using one of the many analytical tools available, such as *What Color Is Your Parachute?* by Richard Bolles, or the Gallup Strengths Finder, and talking to those who know you well. The better we know ourselves, the more we can imagine what kind of work God might be calling us to. The close link between calling and gifting helps us to be contented as we do work that suits us. Contentedness is not particular to our personality type but comes from the knowledge that we are working for God in what he has called us to do. In our ambition to fulfill God-given goals, we can rely on his strength.

Challenging

My former vicar, John Collins, once told me, "Do not settle for black and white if God has given you a vision in color." We should not worry if we feel daunted by what we feel God is calling us to—God-inspired dreams should be challenging. Initially, I was attracted by the money, the opportunity to travel, and the excitement of banking. Alongside that, I became increasingly excited about seeing the kingdom of God grow in a secular society. This vision to see God at the heart of London life has developed and continues to inspire all aspects of my life.

Sir Terry Leahy, the former head of the UK-based supermarket chain Tesco who is widely credited with having built up the Tesco business to its present commanding position, has defined this challenge as follows:

the essence of leadership is painting a vision that others will follow. Find out the truth of the situation, paint a picture of where you want to get to, make a plan and go and do it. It applies to businesses and cities but it also applies to your own personal situation. Always believe that there is a better place and then persuade people to get there with you.[6]

Attainable

Our ambitions should stretch us, but they should also be achievable. I remember the original advertising campaign for Avis, the car rental company. Avis decided that its mission statement would be: "We will be the second largest motor rental company in the world." They knew that Hertz was unassailable as number one. With the slogan "We try harder," it recognized that it could grow its market share to the point where it could challenge Hertz. It was way down the pecking order, so this was a tall but attainable order. We may not achieve all our ambitions, but they should be realistic. "One day, when I am a billionaire, I shall be able to feed millions of people" is a worthy sentiment but is not what I mean by Christian ambition. It is challenging, but is it attainable?

God-Given

Who can forget Eric Liddle's remark in the film *Chariots of Fire* about competing in the 1924 Olympics: "God made me for a purpose. He made me [to be a missionary] for China, but he also made me fast and, when I run, I feel his pleasure."[7] But perhaps the most frequent response we feel when we believe we are being drawn into a new venture is, "Is this really you, God?" It is a good question to ask. We need to know that our ambitions are initiated, sustained, and, where necessary, corrected by God as we step out in faith to do his will.

MARKETING OR MANAGEMENT—HOW DO WE MAKE CAREER CHOICES?

Relationship

Much has been written on the subject of guidance. I myself have struggled to know God's specific will for my life and have talked at length to many at all stages of their working lives as they, too, grapple with the subject. Some of the following practical observations are distilled from these conversations.

> "WE NEED TO KNOW THAT OUR AMBITIONS ARE INITIATED, SUSTAINED, AND, WHERE NECESSARY, CORRECTED BY GOD AS WE STEP OUT IN FAITH TO DO HIS WILL."

As Christians, our main reference point when making decisions is our relationship with God, developed through regular prayer and reading the Bible. A formative verse for me has been Psalm 25:14: "The LORD confides in those who fear him; he makes his covenant known to them."

It is an arresting thought that the Lord of all the world would choose to confide in us. Asking for guidance is, therefore, not wimping out of responsibility or passively accepting the future, but an interactive process. This process deepens our faith. As we bring the impulses of our hearts and our creative ideas to God, we are often given wide choices. However, the language some use when speaking about guidance can imply that we are robots responding to the unchangeable direction of the programmer. I am often skeptical of the introductory phrase "God told me to leave my job." If this is shorthand for a more interactive process, that is wonderful; but it sometimes indicates a misunderstanding of guidance or, worse, a passing of the buck. It is only by accepting responsibility for our actions before God that we mature as human beings.

In many discussions with people leaving university or college and trying to choose from a number of career options, I have found a recurring malaise: paralysis. This paralysis comes from the constant plea for guidance in the expectation that God will make our decisions for us. In some ways it is like trying to enter the door of a vicarage. The vicar says, "After you." In politeness the visitor replies, "After you." "No, no," replies the ever-polite vicar, "after you." "Please, please," says the visitor, "after you." And so it goes on. Guidance can become a revolving door, ever turning, with God expecting us to act and we expecting God to act. However, it is as we move forward and take the first step that we sense God's voice behind us saying, "This is the way; walk in it" (Isaiah 30:21). I have no doubt that God expects us to be the first mover. This was well captured for me in a letter from a financier trying to make a critical decision:

It usually helps to get a bit of motion before I can see where I am going. In a boat, it is difficult to navigate while you are still in the dock, but once out of the harbor, you can feel the currents and the wind and set a course.

—TOSIN ADEREMI, BANKER

I have found it helpful to talk to trusted friends when making big decisions. Some years ago I was sitting at my desk when the telephone rang. I did not recognize the name, but the caller introduced himself as a headhunter. He asked whether I would consider joining another bank in a senior position. He took me to lunch to outline the proposal. There was intense pressure from the headhunter and I could not work out what to do. The attractions of moving were that it was a promotion and financially advantageous. But staying offered the opportunity to grow in a familiar environment in a company with integrity, alongside colleagues who knew both my faults and my strengths. Talking to anyone at work was obviously impossible. Despite my wife's support, I felt very alone in trying to make a major life choice. I called three close friends from church who had some experience in the industry. They offered to meet almost immediately. We talked. I agonized and listened. We prayed. Over time they were able to help me straighten out my thinking. Often the short-term advantages, especially remuneration, can cloud our judgment—and friends can help cut through that by providing an objective viewpoint. Ultimately, the choice and the responsibility for making the choice were mine, but I felt stronger for having talked it through. In the end, I stayed put, which, in retrospect, was the right decision.

When I was thirty-two, I found it difficult to decide whether to ask Fi to marry me. When I prayed, it seemed that God was in the relationship and that he was asking me to take a step of faith but, whenever I reasoned, everything seemed unclear. I rang my father, who told me that a relationship was not a balance sheet, and I would therefore never be able to balance the pros and cons! There were uncertainties that I could not give proper weight to. The idea of commitment frightened me.

One evening Fi and I went to the opera. I still have the program with most of the print on the cover wiped out from the sweat on my palms. We then went out for dinner. I had asked the waiter to have both Perrier water and champagne available. The choice would depend on whether I would pluck up the courage to ask, and of course on what Fi's reply would be. She said yes, the champagne arrived, and the fizzy water wasn't needed! The relief was overwhelming. I felt on top of the world. Almost immediately, however, and for the only time since that night, I doubted the decision. The thought of lifelong commitment suddenly dawned on me. It all seemed too much and I wanted to run for cover.

Forty-eight hours later, Fi and her family wanted to put an engagement announcement in the newspaper. I balked at this idea, preferring to keep things a little more flexible! But deep down I knew the decision was right and there was little point in delaying. The announcement went in! This marked a point of no return, making a step of faith into a public act. Immediately afterward, a huge peace came over me as I realized that God was in that decision. I have never looked back and we are fortunate to have a wonderful marriage.

Timing

You cannot squeeze a fruit ripe. We cannot force something to happen in life if the timing is not right. To the prophet Isaiah, God commented, "I am the LORD; *in its time* I will do this swiftly" (Isaiah 60:22, emphasis added). Often people struggle with the timing of answers to prayers for guidance. We ask ourselves, "Why can't I just press a button and receive an immediate answer?" We want to fast-forward to the conclusion. But the fact is that our perceptions do not change immediately. We need time to distill and consider new insights and, often, a clearer understanding of our motivations filters through the spectrum of everyday activities. As the novelist Julie West observed:

> Even as a child I knew I could write. After a few career diversions where I became distracted by the appeal of earning regular money for such luxuries as rent and food, I finally committed myself to writing at the age of 30. Still in thrall to the concept of actually being paid for my work, I wrote anything that made money: jokes for radio shows, cheesy rhymes or greetings cards, terrible short stories for women's magazines. Eventually I returned to the idea of writing as a calling, a vocation, and began to take it more seriously.
>
> There followed seven fruitless years as I attempted to write my Great Novel, win the Booker Prize, humbly receive the acclaim of the intellectual elite and take my rightful place in literary salons. As I sank into a financial abyss, I experienced every form of publisher's rejection from the tactful to the downright insulting. Then it was time to take stock (the

threatening letters from my bank manager played a valuable part in this decision). Taking a more realistic look at my life made me realize that I had confused the deceptively similar qualities of perseverance and stubbornness.

When I prayed I still believed that God wanted me to be a writer, but felt that my approach might have been wrong. Rather than give up and find a safe nine-to-five job where creativity was smothered at birth, I persevered—but changed my approach. By writing a lighter, more commercial novel, not only did I experience my first success but also the sense that this was what I had been created to do.

I was 40 when I had my first novel published and my sixth book is now due out this year. Perhaps the most telling comment came from a friend who said, "When I read your books, I can hear your voice as clearly as if you were speaking to me in person."

It wasn't the voice I had planned on communicating years ago but, she was right, it was my voice.[8]

If it seems we are being led out of one job into another, it may take time for the groundwork to be prepared. We are sometimes restless for change but may lack the foundations that will sustain a changed set of circumstances. Often a first step is the loosening of the roots that attach us to a particular job. But over time we will also experience a quickening of our spirit in a positive sense, an inclination toward another job or another sector or another way of life. As the one slackens, so the other strengthens. We are not just called out of situations but are called into new openings and challenges. In 1 Corinthians 7:17, Paul wrote, "Retain the place in life that the Lord assigned to [you] and to which God has called [you]." The process of guidance is as important as the guidance itself. That's how we truly learn to trust and to listen.

Signs

Signs from God can help confirm that we are making the right decision. I am often asked if it is right to ask for God to give a sign of guidance. Often a sign comes in the form of God-given peace—not just a sense of relief at a choice made, but also a peace that passes understanding (Philippians 4:7). However, sometimes the sign is more unusual. In the Bible, God tells Gideon that he is to save Israel by his hand. Gideon then twice lays a fleece before the Lord in order to confirm what God had said (Judges 6:36–40). It is important to note that the fleece was laid after the decision to go into battle to save Israel had actually been made—it was not a way of shirking responsibility. Requests for signs should, therefore, be confirmatory (although God may intervene) rather than predictive and need be made only in special cases. Here are a few words from Pippa Richards, a church worker:

> About a year after I became a Christian, I felt that God was calling me out of my management consultant's job, and in to working full-time for my church. The leaders of the church were very keen for me to join the staff, but the problem was there was no immediate opening, or budget to pay me. It was July, and we agreed to review the situation later in the year when the next year's budget was being drawn up.

As time went on I felt that my heart was no longer in my job and it didn't seem fair not to reveal my plans to my boss (let's call him Ben). I was fairly sure that I'd soon either be working for my church or in another ministry. On the other hand, I didn't yet have a firm offer so in a sense there were no plans to tell him. I started to doubt whether I had heard God right, and I prayed each day that he would show me the right time to tell Ben about my longer-term intention.

I became convinced that the "right time" would be after Ben came back from holiday in September.

However, on 11 August, just before he went on holiday, he called a surprise meeting with me to tell me that he was confused. On the one hand, he said I was doing great work. On the other, he was disturbed because he felt that my heart wasn't in the job. "So," he said, "the question I have is: Do you really want to do this job?" My heart was pounding as I thought, *Well, Lord, I suppose this must be the right time, but it's not how I planned it!* So I told him, and we agreed in about five minutes flat when and how I would leave the company. Ben was understanding and supportive, and offered to give me freelance work to bridge any time elapsing between leaving the consultancy and finding my new position.

An hour later, I was sitting alone in the office, in a state of mild shock. It had all happened so quickly. The cat was out of the bag, and suddenly I was heading for a very different life. But was this really God's will, or just a nice idea that I and a few others had dreamed up? I got out my Bible and asked God to please speak to me about this. This had been a really tough week as I'd been dealing with a very difficult situation in my family. If this was God's will, why had he chosen today, of all days, to bring the situation to a head?

My Bible opened at Amos 8 and two verses leapt out at me immediately. The first, verse 2: "The time is ripe for my people Israel." The second, verse 9: "In that day . . . I will make the sun go down at noon and darken the earth in broad daylight."

On that day, 11 August 1999, there had been a total eclipse of the sun just before noon. To me, this was a most wonderful sign of God's presence in the decision and action I'd just taken.

STRATEGIES AND GOALS—HOW DO WE ACHIEVE OUR AMBITIONS?

The musician Artur Schnabel was said to be one of the great pianists in the world because he could keep the image of an entire sonata in his mind while playing every single note. In his book *The Seven Habits of Highly Effective People*, Stephen Covey urges us to start with the end in mind. He wrote, "If the ladder is not leaning against the right wall, every step we take gets us to the wrong place faster."[9] Setting a long view puts our day-to-day work in context.

> "WHEN MAKING DECISIONS, REQUESTS FOR SIGNS FROM GOD SHOULD BE CONFIRMATORY, RATHER THAN PREDICTIVE."

I always advise those who are uncertain about their jobs to treat the work that they are doing as if it were permanent, thus ensuring a long-term attitude. It is also helpful to break up long-term goals into shorter-term objectives. These will need to be reviewed regularly, as our ambitions rarely run along predictable tracks. However, they are still useful, as they are closer in the line of sight and more attainable. For example, to achieve the objective of becoming a director, we have to be prepared to reach our goal in stages. This may mean changing departments strategically, selecting training courses with our goal in mind, and consciously learning management skills from those to whose jobs we aspire.

Steady progress builds confidence to deal with the inevitable setbacks. In Deuteronomy 7:22–23, Moses spoke to the Israelites about the promised land: "The LORD your God will drive out those nations before you, little by little. You will not be allowed to eliminate them all at once, or the wild animals will multiply around you. But the LORD your God will deliver them over to you." To reach our objectives, we often take on too much without being fully prepared. As we proceed in stages, we can eliminate obstacles as we go.

After five years in my first job, I was overlooked for promotion. I felt very let down and wondered whether the senior management was trying to tell me something. Finally, I decided that commitment to any organization is a two-way street: there are obligations on both the employer and the employee. I decided to stay. Careers seldom progress in direct upward lines, but rather in steps and plateaus. Having made my decision, I became more focused in my work, setting myself the goal of being promoted next time around. Ambitions are seldom fulfilled without setbacks, but setbacks are the springboards for achievement. Sometimes we need a paradigm shift in our thinking. We need to think outside the box. The chairman of a European airline company told me that his experience of turning the airline around had been rather like persuading people to run through a brick wall, which they then discovered was made of papier-mâché.

It may be that your particular brick wall is thinner than you think and, once broken, might even be a door of opportunity.

DESTRUCTION AND DECEPTION—HOW DO WE AVOID THE DANGERS?

Lives can be destroyed by ambition that gets out of control. At the end of Shakespeare's play *Henry VIII*, Cardinal Wolsey says to Thomas Cromwell, while on his deathbed: "Had I but served my God with half the zeal I served my King, he would not in mine age have let me naked to mine enemies."[10]

When our ambition becomes divorced from the context of extending God's kingdom, it risks destroying us. In Wolsey's case, serving the king took over from serving God. Similarly, our career can easily become an end in itself if we lose sight of its real purpose. We need to keep acknowledging God as the source of our goals and the director of our lives.

I know people whose ambitions have gotten out of control and destroyed their families and their businesses—as well as themselves. A distinguished consultant told me of the warning signs to look out for: suspicion of other people that borders on paranoia; satisfaction when others fail; indulging in character assassination; introspective behavior; an inability to receive advice or love; egocentricity and the conviction that one is always right; and chronic dissatisfaction with one's life. We need to remember that "The heart is deceitful above all things" (Jeremiah 17:9). Therefore, if we are to hold our ambition lightly and avoid self-deception, we need to ask the Holy Spirit to show us our true intentions. We also need to be accountable to those around us whom we know and trust.

The following questions can be helpful pointers for career direction:

- Do I have confidence when praying and worshipping that God is setting the agenda, or are there persistent niggles?
- Is my ambition so personal that I don't want to talk about it? (This can be a tell-tale sign of self-indulgence.)
- Do other people believe that God is in this vision even if they don't fully grasp it?

If we are satisfied with the answers to these questions, then that is a positive sign.

Donald Bradman, one of the greatest cricketers of all time, used to hit a golf ball with a cricket stump regularly to practice perfecting his eye. Once he had perfected this, it became relatively easy to hit the bigger ball with a wider cricket bat. In our generation, commitment and "stickability" are in short supply, but we need discipline and perseverance in pursuit of our God-given ambitions. Jesus was ambitious to complete the work that God had sent him to do (John 4:34). He listened to the Father constantly and focused entirely on his mission. His last gasp on the cross was, "It is finished" (John 19:30). Our aim also should be to complete the task he has set for us and so to reflect Jesus in our God-given callings.

More than ever before we need Christians with ambition in the workplace—people who will set demanding challenges for themselves but who will also recognize that true ambition cannot be achieved individually. We are to be accountable to others and hold others to account. We also need to break the perception that God prefers us to settle into being low achievers, or we will fail to make an impact on our communities. Paul strained forward to achieve fully an ambition that God gave him. This conviction sustained him throughout every imaginable adversity and enabled him in the end to say he had "fought the good fight," and had "finished the race" (2 Timothy 4:7). That should be our life's mission.

TOUGH DECISIONS

TODAY, WE HAVE MORE KNOWLEDGE THAN EVER BEFORE: WE HAVE access to databases, we can surf the net, we can communicate across continents and make instant connections via Twitter or other social media—but the task of making tricky decisions is no easier. It is so easy to find out the answer to a burning question by looking online—it almost feels as if we cannot live without Google or Wikipedia. Knowledge is instantly accessible. But we are long on knowledge and short on wisdom. Access to mere facts and information does not tell us how to use that knowledge for good: we need wisdom and discernment. How, then, do we make wise, tough decisions at work?

A senior stockbroker once told me that, in his view, it was not possible to hold a general moral view of the workplace. Harsh choices had to be made, compromises reached, and truth had, at times, to be "qualified" because we lived in the real commercial world where everyone knew the game and would not be dealing "as if the workplace were a church." Special rules, therefore, had to be applied to the business world.

I have never accepted this. Medical ethics, cyber ethics, and business ethics describe different areas of choice with differing complexities, but the choices are all based on the same objective biblical standard. There are right and wrong choices. One of the richest men in the ancient world, King Solomon, prayed for "a discerning heart to govern your people and to distinguish between right and wrong" (1 Kings 3:9). All the invented terms such as "inappropriate" and "counterproductive" are efforts to avoid the simple ethical fact that there is a right and wrong course of action that should, without embarrassment, be described as such. This does not mean that there are instant, obvious answers to complex moral questions. On the contrary, there is frequently a process to go through to reach a conclusion. When seeking a compass to navigate through the confusing maze of commercial decisions, I have found four ways of reaching a decision helpful.

First, our relationship with God provides the context for all our decisions. We look to the Bible, which provides a moral framework for our actions. Second, we have God-given faculties of reasoning underlined throughout the Bible, and demonstrated by the prophet Isaiah's call: "Come now, let us reason together" (Isaiah 1:18). Third, we are given what Augustine called "a kind of silent clamour of truth ringing inside"[1]—our conscience. This is the Spirit prodding us in a God-ward direction. Last, we need to assess the consequences of our decisions, not only for ourselves but also for others. The best decisions are made when these four are aligned.

DECISIONS AND VALUES—HOW TO BE CONSISTENT

Making tough decisions is one of the most crucial issues in the workplace. We need to be clear, robust, and determined in making our choices. Of course, everyone makes decisions based, sometimes unconsciously, on a set of values. There is often a tacit assumption at work that we all share a set of common values, but this may not be the case.

> A client asked me to pass some vital information about his business to the underwriter. I forgot to pass it on, resulting in a very restrictive decision from the underwriter regarding my client's insurance policy and a very annoyed client. My initial reaction was to hide the fact that this was my mistake. It would have been easy to pass it off as the underwriter's neglect and I spent a while trying to work out the best way to do this. However, as I did so, I became aware of a growing sense of shame. I realized, having prayed under my breath, that the only thing to do was to risk the client's anger and tell him that the mistake was mine. So I rang him and confessed. His response surprised me: "Don't worry—if you never make mistakes that just shows that you never do anything." I have learned a lot from this one, and have become more confident about living out my values in the workplace.
>
> —PAUL GROVES, INSURANCE BROKER

At the heart of all business scandals is an individual exercising a judgment on what is right and wrong but also, sadly, of what can be gotten away with. There is a need for regulation, but these rules of the game are merely a guide and not a substitute for a set of faith-based values. Like our faith, our values will affect our decisions in every area of our lives. In this sense there is no distinction between so-called personal decisions and work-related decisions. Integrity is the word we use when our actions are aligned with our principles and there is no disconnection between the two. This comes into sharp focus when the values that public figures live by are seen to differ from those they promote. The UK parliamentary expenses scandal of 2009 had this issue at its core. The 2008–09 global financial crisis undermined Western claims of leadership, not just in politics and business, but in morals as well. It was not Chinese, or Brazilian, or Indian financial institutions that pushed the world to the brink of disaster. It was the Western financial institutions, the Western governments and regulators, and the Western consumers. The question of values seems to never have been more urgent or more important. We cannot compartmentalize our lives into a private sphere and a professional sphere, with separate rules for each.

A few years ago I went to Italy representing my company on a trip organized by a major client. One evening ten of us (all men) went out for dinner and then on to a club. It became clear that the guy organizing the evening had arranged for female escorts for all of us at the next venue. As I realized what was happening, I had to act quickly to avoid being carried along by the crowd and into the next taxi. I subtly escaped to the gents and called my wife for some moral support and time to think. Then

I was able to catch a taxi back to the hotel. The next morning I definitely felt excluded. One guy commented to me, "Whatever plays away stays away," and I felt he was looking for reassurance that I wouldn't spill the beans. Others gave the impression that they found my non-participation slightly pathetic. Still others, I think,

> "WE CANNOT COMPARTMENTALIZE OUR LIVES INTO A PRIVATE SPHERE AND A PROFESSIONAL SPHERE, WITH SEPARATE RULES FOR EACH."

felt judged. All in all, though it was the right thing to do, it had an adverse effect on my relationship with these people, in some cases long-term. However, one guy who noticed my stance has recently sought opportunities to work with me.

—ALEX LEE, FINANCE DIRECTOR

PRACTICAL STEPS—HOW DO WE MAKE WISE CHOICES?

1. Follow the wisdom of God

Wisdom, which comes from God, is knowing and doing what is right. This is how wisdom is described in the introduction to Proverbs in *The Message*, Eugene Peterson's modern translation of the Bible:

"Wisdom" is the biblical term for this on-earth-as-it-is-in-heaven everyday living. Wisdom is the art of living skillfully

in whatever actual conditions we find ourselves. It has virtu-
ally nothing to do with information as such, with knowledge
as such. A college degree is no certification of wisdom—nor
is it primarily concerned with keeping us out of moral mud
puddles, although it does have a profound moral effect upon us.

Wisdom has to do with becoming skillful in honoring
our parents and raising our children, handling our money
and conducting our sexual lives, going to work and exercising leadership, using words well and treating friends kindly,
eating and drinking healthily, cultivating emotions within
ourselves and attitudes toward others that make for peace.
Threaded through all these items is the insistence that the
way we think of and respond to God is the most practical
thing we do. In matters of everyday practicality, nothing,
absolutely nothing, takes precedence over God.[2]

Through reading the Bible regularly and meditating on
God's truth, we build up reservoirs of wisdom and form a biblical
worldview.

Our own reflections can be supplemented by reading about
other Christians, whose experiences provide useful case studies
of following God's actions in different situations. Building strong
foundations in this way stands us in good stead for moments
when we need to make difficult decisions and stops us thumbing
through our Bible as if it were Google, desperately looking for a
quick answer.

When facing a critical choice, our first response should be
to step back. It can be difficult to create space when a dominant

issue is at the forefront of our mind. I recommend that people facing a major decision take two days to seek God. Day one is simply to chill out. It is amazing how draining it is to confront a looming decision. A break to restore physical strength is therefore essential. During day two it is better not to pray constantly about the particular decision. Rather, use the time to meditate on who God is, on his ways in the world generally, and on his overall plans for his people. This search for a wider context alleviates the acute pressure caused by constantly churning a decision around in our minds. It also widens perspective and enables the decision to be made from a broader point of view—God's point of view. We need constant reminders that his thoughts are not our thoughts, nor his ways our ways (Isaiah 55:8). The decision will then be clearer and we will be able to implement it from a place of rest. (Ideally I would suggest taking two days, but this may not always be possible. Taking whatever time you can is the important factor.)

I remember being approached by a major international bank to join them. There were certain compelling features to this initiative. First, it was flattering to be headhunted. Second, financially there was the attraction of a better package, and that felt good. But there was a niggle that I could not define—a certain unease that seemed to want to hold me back from doing that which, on paper, sounded entirely sensible. The decision was complicated by my position in the bank and the effect that leaving would have on other people at a time when the morale was low. The title sounded good. The remit was bigger and better, but the day-to-day questions that we all have to face when making decisions concerning moving jobs—who we will report to, who our colleagues will be—needed to be given weight greater than my initial enthusiasm. These factors determine whether we will be happy or not. In all major decisions, there are many factors to consider. What is vital is that consideration is given to each of them. It was when I weighed up various alternatives that my concern relating to the nature of the structure of the management of the new firm was greater than the other attractions. When I applied this weight, the doubts began to grow.

I therefore took a day off to be alone (I hate being alone) to walk along the Thames near Henley where I had previously spent time when facing a difficult decision. I don't know what it is but sometimes there are places that one is drawn to by the memories of having heard God in that place. I made the conscious decision not to analyze the particular issue by running through the pros and cons, but instead to seek God's broader wisdom. The aim was to take my focus off myself and to seek God's wisdom. I wanted to take that time to consciously listen for his voice and to reaffirm my desire to do his will. I came back with a far better weighting on the different choices that had to be made. As a result, a certain peace took hold of me and the decision not to take the new appointment was made almost effortlessly, having loomed anxiously before.

2. Make the complex simple

Our ability to make tough decisions improves with our technical competence. We do need to understand the technicalities of our job, but there is a real temptation to confuse technical complexity with the underlying fundamental choices, which are often simple. In the words of a senior US Army figure, the late General Omar Bradley, "We have become a nation of technological giants and moral pygmies."[3]

> I work in child protection, and the most difficult decision I face is to decide when a child needs to be removed from his or her home. I had one particularly complex case, which I agonized over for some time. My decision was subsequently challenged in court, which I found very stressful, but eventually the court backed my judgment and supported my decision. I realized that I did actually have the necessary skills to do my job and make these decisions. It's never easy, but I feel more confident as a result of the court case.
>
> —VANESSA CLARK, SOCIAL WORKER

When I have to make a difficult decision at work, I try to reduce it to its simplest form. It can be helpful to write down the issue, using the minimum number of words. Most complex decisions have at their root simple—albeit difficult—choices. It can take time to see the real choice in its stark simplicity, stripped of mountains of fact, others' opinions, our own reflections, and confused motivation. How often does one hear in a meeting, "But the *real* question is . . ."?

3. Listen to the question

In our day-to-day work, we have to deal with a range of questions. It is therefore instructive to see how Jesus dealt with three different yet equally difficult questions in Luke 20.

In the first case, Jesus was teaching the people in the temple. The senior community leaders approached him and asked, "Tell us by what authority you are doing these things. . . . Who gave you this authority?" (v. 2). Jesus, of course, saw that they were trying to trick him and replied by asking a question: "Tell me, John's baptism—was it from heaven, or from [human origin]?" (vv. 3–4). The questioners were now caught in a dilemma. If they said "from heaven," then why didn't they believe him? But if they replied "of human origin," they feared being stoned because John was generally thought to be a prophet. They prevaricated, answering, "We don't know where it was from" (v. 7). Jesus therefore declined to answer their question. Not *every* question has to be answered. It is important to remember this, for example, when conducting a negotiation on behalf of a client. An unfair question, such as, "Is this really your client's final offer?" is usually best avoided by saying something like, "This is the offer that is on the table for your consideration."

In the second case, Jesus gave an extremely adroit answer. The teachers of the law and the chief priests sent spies to try to catch Jesus out. They said to him, "Teacher, we know that you speak and teach what is right, and that you do not show partiality but teach the way of God in accordance with the truth. Is it right for us to pay taxes to Caesar or not?" (vv. 21–22). In the first sentence the spies were buttering him up. It is like the salesman sitting in a meeting and hearing a customer say, "I think this is the best product we have ever seen. It does everything for us. It is so good, our clients just can't wait to get more of it." Then comes the sting in the tail: "But the price . . ." In Jesus' story the sting is the question, "Is it right for us to pay taxes to Caesar or not?" It was set up so that Jesus would either be accused of treason (if he said taxes should not be paid) or seen as an oppressor of the people for siding with Caesar (if he said they should). Jesus avoided both. He asked them for a coin and pointed out Caesar's portrait, replying, "Then give to Caesar what is Caesar's, and to God what is God's" (v. 25). Just because we are presented with a polarity of the questioner's own choice, we do not have to restrict our answers to the options offered. In a work situation we often feel forced into a yes or no answer when the issue is best approached from a different angle.

Third, the Sadducees asked a particularly complicated question about a woman with seven husbands, inquiring whose wife she would be when she got to heaven (vv. 27–33). It is a difficult but honest question and Jesus gave them a helpful and clear reply. When the real object of the question is to elicit a straight answer, then one should be given. One of the distinguishing features of a good adviser is the ability to develop a trusting relationship with a client. This is ultimately tested in the willingness to say no to a proposed transaction and to give honest advice to a client. For many years, Grand Metropolitan Hotels, one of the largest hotels and spirits groups in the world, had its eyes on the brewing company Guinness. I remember working with the team to advise Grand Metropolitan that it would have been inappropriate to acquire Guinness at this point. It was a simple question. Was it the right timing from the point of view of the shareholders of both companies, the macro-economic climate, and the trading positions of the companies? Simple, but complex. Although it would have been significantly remunerative for us to push the deal, we decided not to do so and to advise against the deal being done for a number of reasons. I am reminded of the saying of Karl Barth that we should strive for simplicity at the end of complexity.

The trust between the client and ourselves was, if anything, strengthened. A few years later when the timing changed, better valuations existed, and markets were in a better state, we advised in favor of a merger. The merger took place to create Diageo, one of the largest consumer products companies in the world. I recall the meetings with the chief executive and his saying, "Well if you didn't think it is right then and you do think it's right now, then I trust your advice."

So to three different kinds of questions we hear three different kinds of answers. The first is a trick question, which Jesus did not answer. The second is a complex question set up to be a trap, which Jesus discerned and avoided. The third is an honest question that got an honest answer. We need the help of the Holy Spirit to discern the nature of the question.

> "IT IS IMPORTANT NOT TO ASK A QUESTION IF YOU ARE UNABLE TO HANDLE THE ANSWER."

It is important not to ask a question if you are unable to handle the answer. A client told me the story of Robert McNamara, secretary of state in America at the time of the Cuban missile crisis, who was reflecting on a conversation with Andrei Gromyko, the foreign minister of Russia.

McNamara had deliberately avoided asking Gromyko the direct question, "Are there nuclear missiles on Cuba?" He was confident the foreign minister would not lie to him and that therefore the answer would be "Yes." A positive reply might well have led to an immediate attack. Wisely, he did not ask the question, because the implications of the answer were too hot to handle—the crisis was averted and perhaps this restraint contributed to the outcome. A different question could have elicited a different outcome.

4. Consider the consequences

Many tough decisions that have to be made each day in the workplace require us to measure the short-term implications against the longer-term. So, for example, spending money in the short term might be painful, but in the longer term the investment could well pay off. Decisions are destroyed by "short-termism." A clear example of this is the recent financial crisis, where short-term decisions made by banks practically wrecked the world's financial system. We need to cultivate the habit of making immediate tough decisions in light of future circumstances. Jesus said, "Suppose one of you wants to build a tower. Will [you] not first sit down and estimate the cost to see if [you have] enough money to complete it?" (Luke 14:28).

When we are making a difficult decision, it is more important to look carefully at what could potentially go wrong, rather than focusing on the potential benefits or profit. We should manage the downside risk and let the upside take care of itself. Too much time is usually spent thinking about the potential benefits when it is the potential cost of things going wrong that needs most careful attention. The impact of our decisions on other people should also be considered.

> Last year my business reached the point where I could no longer avoid making some of my workforce redundant. It was a very, very painful experience, one of the toughest decisions I ever made. I was constrained by the requirements of employment law but tried to be both fair and compassionate to each individual. I prayed that each one would quickly find a new job that would suit their gifting and meet their family's financial needs.
>
> —RAY WILKINSON, HUMAN RESOURCES MANAGER

5. Implement the strategy

Once we have made a decision, we need to think about the best way to implement it. Our call as Christians is to be "as shrewd as snakes and as innocent as doves" (Matthew 10:16). This is one of the biggest challenges of the Christian life, especially as I believe that we are called to be both shrewd and innocent at the *same* time.

In the parable of the shrewd manager (Luke 16:1–9), the manager is shrewd, yet dishonest, but only his shrewdness is commended. Our challenge is to be shrewd, by which I mean streetwise, clever, or strategic, while at the same time honest. When Daniel was taken to the Babylonian court, he resolved not to defile himself with the non-kosher royal food and wine given by the king (Daniel 1). However, rather than giving a flat refusal, he approached the chief official for permission to have a vegetarian diet instead. Daniel knew that the official would be executed if those in his charge did not look well. Rather than force a confrontation, he suggested a trial period of ten days. The special diet would continue only if they all looked well. By considering the situation from the official's point of view, taking his concerns seriously and providing a pragmatic course of action, Daniel was able to get what he wanted. God blessed him and made him stronger than any of the others.

PROFIT AND RESPONSIBILITY—CAN WE HAVE BOTH?

One of the most difficult areas for decision is how to balance the needs of the wider communities in which businesses operate with the pursuit of profit. For many, the idea that a corporation should try to embrace a wider agenda is a breach of a fundamental understanding of the need to maximize profit for the benefit of shareholders. But, increasingly, there is recognition of the importance of the wider perspective, alongside a necessarily strong defense of profit. This is seen in there having been an upsurge in corporate social responsibility in major companies' strategies over the last decade. After all, only profitable, efficient firms will have the added value to share more widely. With the right to make profit afforded by a free market economy comes the responsibility to do so ethically. The twin of rights is duties. Too often we assert our rights but neglect the acceptance of a reciprocal duty. Employers recognize that not just shareholders—but also consumers, customers, pensioners, and the community in which the corporation operates—are stakeholders affected by corporate decisions.

My own view is that properly developed corporate responsibility, far from being a drag on profitability, is essential to long-term stability. If major corporations act responsibly and out of a sense of being good global citizens, much of the friction caused by relations between the developing and developed world will be mitigated. If we wish to spread the benefits of globalization as widely as possible, free trade will also need to become fair trade. The failure of the World Trade Organization to deal with the subsidies given by developed nations to their own exporters, and the tariffs imposed on the developing world when seeking markets in developed countries, are deeply offensive. This failure creates a two-tier system favoring developed nations over those trying to develop their own economies. The cries of the disenchanted should call us to devise a globalization that serves all—and is seen to serve all.

A robust concern for the environment is also key. The beginning of Genesis makes it clear that God has made human beings stewards of the material resources of the earth. I would argue that the capitalist system, with all its faults, is still the best system for utilizing these resources, but efficiency should not outweigh sustainability. These issues of corporate responsibility are relevant for all employees, not just those in positions of senior executive authority. Often I'm told, "It's okay for you, but no one will listen to me." All employers want their businesses to be thought of as places of excellence and best practice. Increasingly, there are representative groups and committees in which it would be appropriate for employees at every level to raise these matters. The more concern that is shown for these issues, the more responsive management will become to them. The culture is changing and the time has come to draw together the short-term requirements of the marketplace with some of the more important long-term effects of globalization.

We also have a responsibility toward people. It is important for all employees to know that they are valued, irrespective of their gender, marital status, nationality, faith, background, or sexual orientation. Diversity provides a range of different perspectives, which brings a better balance of judgment to a team. We are all made in the image of God and, therefore, have something to offer. When Christ came, he broke down the barriers that divide people (Ephesians 2:14), and working together is one way of living this out. It is also important for employees to be able to respect the values of their organization.

For me it was an enormous advantage to work for a bank that consistently set integrity as its hallmark. I always knew that my values would be given a fair hearing and evaluated on their merits. When I was a junior executive, I remember a debate about whether it was appropriate to sponsor the financing of a series of clinics primarily focused on abortion. Instinctively I felt it was wrong, but I knew that others disagreed. The simple option was to say nothing, but I decided to speak to the chairman and explain the level of my concerns, which related both to my personal morality and to the reputation of the bank. To my surprise he thought that it was appropriate to raise both aspects. At the critical meeting I prayed that we would not have to make the decision and thus be forced into division. The proposal fell away for an apparently unrelated reason, but it was right to raise the issue. Of course, not every moral issue has to be fought with the same moral intensity. Defective work practices often require time and patient argument to be corrected. Discernment is needed in order to know when to press an issue and when to stay silent. Above all, respect for others who have a different point of view should be paramount.

PATTERNS OF LIVING—WHO SHAPES THEM?

We are overwhelmed by choices in everyday life. It is an essential part of our spiritual journey that we learn to make difficult choices and then to live with their consequences. Making decisions is a prime part of our maturing as people. We don't always get it right, however hard we may have prayed and sought God's help—we are human and not divine. And yes, we rejoice in getting judgments right, but let us not forget that we cannot gain experience without making mistakes and taking wrong decisions. But wisdom is greater than experience. And we grow in wisdom only if we learn from our mistakes. Siegmund Warburg, my first boss, said on this subject: "Some name it disappointment and become poorer, others name it experience and become richer."[4]

Our decisions should be made from the perspective of lives lived for God and not just for our own enjoyment.

Paul, writing to the Romans, urges us not to let the pressures from the world shape our pattern of living. He gave this summary, which I have found foundational to my decision making:

> So here's what I want you to do, God helping you: Take your everyday, ordinary life—your sleeping, eating, going-to-work, and walking-around life—and place it before God as an offering. Embracing what God does for you is the best thing you can do for him. Don't become so well-adjusted to your culture that you fit into it without even thinking. Instead, fix your attention on God. You'll be changed from the inside out. Readily recognize what he wants from you, and quickly respond to it. Unlike the culture around you, always dragging you down to its level of immaturity, God brings the best out of you, develops well-formed maturity in you. (Romans 12:1–2 THE MESSAGE)

FIVE

WORK–LIFE BALANCE

HOW OFTEN DO YOU HEAR THE FRUSTRATED CRY, "I HAVEN'T GOT enough time"? The pressure to do an increasing number of activities more and more rapidly is all-pervasive, but we do not become holy by working harder or doing more. There are proper restraints that need to be placed upon our work. Work–life balance is now at the top of many human resources departments' agenda. It is clear that the demands made on people to devote huge amounts of time to work for an undefined period are unsustainable. The owner of a large international French-based spirits company told me that he had offered his employees the opportunity to exchange the notoriously long French holidays for a lump sum in cash. While those in their forties accepted the offer at once, those in their twenties rejected it. A younger generation is increasingly, and rightly, seeking a lifestyle that balances life in the workplace and outside it. Unlike their parents' generation, they are not willing to sacrifice time with family and friends for their work.

COMPETING DEMANDS—WHAT SHOULD OUR PRIORITIES BE?

Priorities are essential if we are to achieve our ambitions and at the same time hold on to our values. I believe that the right order of priorities is that God should come first, our core relationships second, and the work that God has called us to third. For most people, core relationships will either be with their spouse and children or close friendships, and the work that God has called them to will primarily be their jobs, but may include other God-given activities. Although keeping this balance right is difficult, we may be surprised when putting our priorities in the right order:

> I was in charge of the emerging market debt financing business for a large investment bank in London. My main focus was on Latin America. I really loved my work as it brought me into contact with very senior people in governments and companies in these emerging countries. Although the traveling and working hours were demanding, it was worthwhile. I felt we were contributing to the economic development of these countries.
>
> One afternoon I received some very exciting news at work. We had made it to the final stages of a bidding contest for a $200 million financing for a Brazilian company, our first in that country. We stood to make substantial fees and

establish our credentials in a huge market that we had not yet cracked. I rushed home to spend a bit of time with my wife and our three-month-old baby girl. A lengthy conference call was scheduled at 8:00 P.M. with the board of the Brazilian company. I was going to explain our proposed strategy for raising the money and answer a barrage of questions. Half an hour later they would choose the bank they wanted to work with. I arrived home full of excitement, only to have my wife, Debs, hand me the baby and her bottle.

"Here," she said. "I'm so glad you're on time because I need to go to my dinner right away."

"What dinner?"

"You know, Gill [Debs's boss] is in town from San Francisco for just one day and we're having dinner with all of the staff. Don't tell me you forgot."

"I forgot," I said sheepishly. "And I have a call with the Brazilians in an hour to finalize this deal. If I can't be on the call, we'll lose the business."

I felt like throwing a tantrum but, in all honesty I knew it wasn't fair for Debs to be three hours late for her dinner. I took Lily in my arms and prayed for something to work out. I was not very hopeful.

Forty-five minutes later the telephone rang. I was playing peek-a-boo with Lily. When I tried to start the conference call, Lily started wailing at eighty-five decibels. I tried to get Sergio, the finance director, to pick up the phone so the others couldn't hear our conversation, but he would not take my hints. "Sergio, I'm sorry I can't talk to you now. It is absolutely impossible," I said, with two of my team in New York and another in Sao Paolo listening, as well as his entire board.

"Miles, you have to speak to us now. We are about to make our decision."

"I can't. Is there any way we can delay?"

"No, we can't! I told you this afternoon. What is the problem?"

"Uh," I hesitated. Then I decided to tell the truth. "I made a big mistake. My wife is out tonight—I completely forgot about a dinner she has with her boss. I really messed up. I am looking after my baby girl right now. She is crying so I really should go. I am terribly sorry for any disappointment this may have caused you. I understand that you have to make the contribution I had hoped to make."

"Baby girl? What's her name?"

"Lily."

"That's a pretty name." I heard murmurs of approval in the background. "Is that her crying right now?"

"Yes. I am so sorry about this."

"Don't worry about it. How long do you need?"

"I'll put her to bed in about an hour."

"Call us when she's asleep. We'll be here."

I hung up, completely dumbfounded. I sang to Lily until she went to sleep, and then called the Brazilians. I did not dare to hook in my colleagues in New York because I feared their scathing criticism for being willing to blow a deal over a ridiculous babysitting problem. Sergio and the whole board were still there.

"Well, is she asleep?" he asked.

"Yes, she is," I replied, feeling like a complete idiot.

"That's good. Okay, what do you want to tell us?"

I went through our proposal. It was the most amazing conversation. I put any thought of closing the deal out of my mind. All I wanted to do was help these people through their concerns and issues so that they could make the decision that worked best for their company. Eventually, they hung up to deliberate. Half an hour later they called me back to say we had won the business. I just sat there and looked at the phone. I left an embarrassed message for my colleagues in New York to start cranking up the machine, and went to bed, thanking God for helping me out.

—MILES PROTTER, MANAGING
PARTNER OF THE VALUES PARTNERSHIP

Early on in my working life, I found it hard to imagine what it would look like to be committed to my work and yet give my core relationships higher priority. A crunch point came when I found myself utterly absorbed in a stimulating and confidential deal. I became so engrossed that I didn't speak to my wife, Fi, for a week. She was extremely patient but, not surprisingly, by the end of the week felt desperately neglected. I had to resist the temptation toward self-justification. As I did so, I knew that this was not the right way to live and I resolved that this would never happen again.

As I travel a great deal, I now try to speak to Fi every day, wherever I am in the world. I avoid waking her up wherever possible, but we have decided together that being woken is preferable to not speaking. The main point of the phone call is to show that Fi has my front of mind and heart's attention, and for this it is important to stay in touch through a daily exchange of information.

I also try to stay in regular contact with my children, even if it is just a quick text message to support them in whatever it is they are involved in. When I am in the middle of an impossibly busy period and it seems that I will never have the time or inclination to have fun again, this is the moment to put something in the diary. At times, we need counterbalancing stimuli. We also need reminders of key relationships and the need to maintain them.

I appreciate the support of a small group of friends that meets regularly to keep in touch and pray. I have also valued mentors over the years, generally older Christians, who have been kind enough to offer me their time and wisdom. I have limited interest in listening to work–life balance theories, but I do want to learn from those who are engaging with the issue and making progress. We all need to help each other. It is experience, and not the textbook, that makes the difference.

YES OR NO—HOW DO WE DECIDE?

The writer Arnold Bennett remarked, "We shall never have more time. We have, and always have had, all the time there is."[1] Who is the master of time? Either time imposes its tyranny on our lives or we act decisively, using it to reflect our priorities. Instead of trying to slot God into a predispositioned spreadsheet of our own making, we need to shape our lives into his patterns because we realize these are good for us. We need to exercise the authority that God has given us over time, recognizing the forces that distract us from fulfilling God's purposes. This requires more and more discipline with the unremitting distraction of social media and smartphones.

Once, while I was at a breakfast meeting with a new business developer for a multinational corporation, we discussed the issue of planning. He traveled a lot with his job, but he told me that he tries to organize his time so that he is home on weekends

> "WE SHALL NEVER HAVE MORE TIME. WE HAVE, AND ALWAYS HAVE HAD, ALL THE TIME THERE IS."
> —ARNOLD BENNETT

to see his family and on Tuesday evenings to go to the church group he and his wife feel called to lead together. This involves a bit of planning and sometimes leaving for work on some very late flights after the Tuesday evening group has ended.

I recall a story told of the best banker of his generation, Sir Siegmund Warburg. His secretary rushed in to tell him that the Chancellor of the Exchequer was on the telephone and said it was urgent. Sir Siegmund's reply was instructive: "Urgent for whom? For him or for me?" This was perhaps a little arrogant but it proves a point. As stewards of time we need to step back and ensure that we are not merely whirled along by the exigencies of the moment. The urgent is often the enemy of the important.

The story of Jesus in John 11:1–16 is very telling. His great friend Lazarus was sick and on the point of death. Every instinct in him must have been driving him to go and see his friend. But Jesus waited and did not rush off immediately as his disciples would have urged him to do. In due course, he decided the time was right to go, even though Lazarus had already died by the time he arrived. But at first he held back. At times we need to check powerful and natural emotions in order to achieve God-given objectives. The first gut reaction is not necessarily the right course of action. Jesus knew the bigger picture and ultimately was able to glorify God by going at the right time and raising Lazarus from the dead.

Jesus did only what he saw the Father doing (John 5:19). In our work the temptation can be to try to do more than God is doing. I often have to remind myself that I can do only what God's will is for me, and no more. Restraint is an important understanding of priority. We need to say no in order to be able to say yes.

> "WE NEED TO SAY NO IN ORDER TO BE ABLE TO SAY YES."

A few years ago, I was asked to be a trustee of a major charity. I loved the people involved and believed in their vision. I was flattered by the request, and everything within me was ready to say yes. However, while praying, I felt a lingering uncertainty. The balance of work and other commitments meant that, reluctantly, I had to say no. It is hard to say no when you want to say yes. But saying no to one thing often opens the way to another. Subsequent events proved the decision right, as the time commitment would have been far greater than originally anticipated, and more than I could have managed.

Learning to refuse the excessive demands of the workplace can feel daunting. Many of us feel we need a worthy excuse, such as a family wedding or a pre-booked weekend away, to justify saying no to extra work. However, when we take a step back, all of us can see that rest is essential. I aim for at least a day a week when I switch off from the creative activity of my mainstream work. Keeping one day free of work is healthy—and modeled by God in the work of creation. We should respect it but not be bound legalistically by it (Mark 2:27). Like many others, I sometimes have to spend Sunday working, but it is important that this happens by exception, and not because we are failing to plan our work, falling into bad habits, or becoming ill-disciplined in our work patterns. Learning to work efficiently, and without time wasting, is an important biblical principle that enables us to develop the necessary discipline to become good stewards of time. Most companies know the negative impact of making ill-considered demands on employees. When it does occur, a well-reasoned discussion with a manager is a good approach.

Balance often needs two people to strike the pivotal point. Making our concerns known with a direct but positive attitude often has the benefit not only of resolving a particular work–life imbalance but also of affecting working practices for the good, thus benefiting other colleagues.

COMPULSIONS AND ADDICTIONS— HOW CAN WE BREAK FREE?

To many today the word *idol* is associated with the cult of celebrity, something benign like the TV show *American Idol*. However, in the Bible, an idol is anything that pushes God out of our lives. Compulsions and addictions such as workaholism or alcoholism, shopping binges, Internet pornography, and recreational drugs are all idols. Only God can break the power of destructive habits and bring balance to our lives.

I remember praying with a young stockbroker at the end of a church service. He reluctantly told me that he was addicted to cocaine. He felt that there had to be more to life but God seemed inaccessible to him. We talked about the fact that on the cross Jesus broke the power of evil, including all compulsions and addictions. When I prayed for him, the Holy Spirit came upon him with extraordinary power, causing him to shake visibly. He subsequently joined a home group and, although at times it was a struggle to stay clean, the drug dependency was broken, leaving him free to live a fulfilled and balanced life.

> "WORKAHOLISM CAN BE AS ACUTE AN ADDICTION AS ANY RECREATIONAL SUBSTANCE."

A senior executive told me that his greatest struggle as a Christian was his reliance on work to give meaning to his life. Workaholism can be as acute an addiction as any recreational substance. As we talked, we discovered that many of the root causes of his issue seemed to lie in his childhood, where he had been under constant pressure to achieve. Somehow, whatever he did was not good enough for his father. We prayed together and he accepted that there was a problem, thus clearing the decks for a life strategy. He knew that, if he did not bring his addiction under control, it could well destroy his life and his marriage, and he decided to take responsibility for restoring the balance. We agreed on some strategies, including not taking papers and problems home, working efficiently during the day, not talking about work to his wife for a period, and practicing doing nothing. He found the latter the most difficult of all but started to keep Sundays free not only from work but also from thinking about work. Gradually he started to realize that he did not need to work to be valued by God. Jesus heard the Father's voice saying, "You are my Son, whom I love; with you I am well pleased" (Luke 3:22), before any of his public work had begun. Love precedes work.

Over the years I have had the privilege to observe that, as the overall balance of this senior executive's life has changed, he has become fulfilled and at ease in his relationships not only at home but particularly at work.

In an interview in *Fortune*, Daniel Vassela, the chief executive of one of the largest pharmaceutical companies in the world—Novartis—was asked about money and motivation:

The strange part is this, the more I made, the more I got preoccupied with money. When suddenly I didn't have to think about money as much, I found myself starting to think increasingly about it. Money corrupts the mind. By the same token, you can find yourself in a situation where you worry more and more about your reputation and become its prisoner. It is wrong to worry about whether you will be the hero next month. One day, the glitter will be gone anyway.[2]

I remember talking to a twenty-five-year-old banker who had just received a big bonus and realized that he had become more absorbed with the money than he had expected. The apostle Peter wrote in his second letter that people are slaves to whatever has mastered them (2 Peter 2:19). A love of money or power can grow almost imperceptibly until we find ourselves enslaved. My own experience is that freedom from such captivity requires daily discipline. We need to recognize and be grateful for God's hand in what we have achieved, and not be afraid to use our money, reputation, and skill for his purposes. But we also need to pray regularly for the power of God's Spirit to dethrone idols that rob us of our freedom.

FREEDOM AND DISCIPLINE—HOW DO WE GET THE TREND LINE RIGHT?

In practice it is not possible to lead a perfectly balanced life all the time. There are phases in many careers that demand long hours: for example, the early years of medicine. In addition, all of us have times when the demands of work outstrip our desire to live balanced lives.

The barrister in a difficult trial will be consumed for a number of weeks with the issues. A business trip may take us away for a period. At other times family life will be of critical importance: for example, when a baby is born, a child starts a new school, or someone close to us is sick. But what is important is not the oscillations but the trend. Is it directionally right, even if momentarily out of line? For example, if the trend line shows an excess of time spent on church activities, then it should be corrected in the next period to allow for more time at work or with family.

Within a well-organized schedule we must also allow time for sudden changes of pace. New projects arrive unexpectedly or God intervenes in our lives in a way that needs a response. If we don't have flexibility, our life can be driven by fixed priorities and burdensome milestones. The Spirit of God brings freedom within a framework. This is the balance we seek. Jesus talks to those who are burnt out and urges them to discover "the unforced rhythms of grace" (Matthew 11:29 THE MESSAGE). We each need to work out a style of time management that suits us. The test is this: Does the structure free us or trap us?

We should review our diaries rigorously: How much time have I spent productively? How much has been wasted? Have I given myself enough time to rest? Have I managed to spend regular time alone with God? Can I see what God is blessing and then resource it with time, energy, and money? Often these questions are easier to answer with the help of some close friends. With God, we try to draw the right line, realizing that mistakes will be made along the way. The diary review is good because the record does not lie. It tells it as it is. The next step is to try to plan the forward diary to reflect your chosen lifestyle values. If you constantly fail the diary audit, then it's time to think again. Something is out of kilter in your life.

STOP AND THINK—REVIEW TO RENEW

On the highway of God's purposes, it is a waste of time to be constantly looking for the exit or worrying as to whether we are on track. We need not worry daily whether a previous decision is the right one or what the next move should be. It is in this sense that Jesus warns us that we should take care of each day as it comes, for it has problems of its own, and not to fret about tomorrow (Matthew 6:34). However, many people carry on doing the same work uncritically. They stay busy but bored. To avoid this, all of us need to review our lives from time to time, for example on key birthdays or at regular set intervals.

> Each year I had an annual appraisal as part of my pay review process. I found this was very helpful in terms of recognizing what I had learned and achieved to date and seeing where I wanted to go. Preparing for my review one year, I realized that I was in the wrong career. I looked at my senior colleagues—their lifestyle, responsibilities, and ambitions— and realized I did not want their jobs. I am glad to have been given the opportunity to stop and think about my work from a

professional standpoint and would counsel an annual review to everyone. I did have to wait a few years before I was called into something new, but the review helped me see where my strengths and passions lie.

—JULIE BRANT, SOLICITOR

Sometimes fundamental doubts about what we are doing hit us unexpectedly. There are times—such as when we are hitting the big numbers such as thirty, forty, or fifty—when it is right to reassess one's career and check up on the many crosswinds that can drive us off course from our original objectives. I remember after several years in the same job being involved in the battle for control of Harrods—one of the most hard-fought battles in UK corporate history. We were advising the company, which was being attacked by another company headed by Tiny Rowland, a well-known but controversial entrepreneur. It was a lengthy and exhausting transaction and I found myself questioning whether I really wanted to spend the rest of my life working to achieve the corporate objectives of others. I reopened a book I thought I had closed and again asked whether I might be called to a full-time preaching ministry. I concluded that this should not be dismissed as a consequence of stress but that it was a proper question that went deeper.

When I turned forty, I reanalyzed the reasons why I was in my job at the time and spoke to a prominent Christian leader who knew me well. I was surprised by the strength of his reaction as he advised me to stay where I was. He pointed out that my original sense of God's calling was unchanged, and questioned whether I had just hit what he called the "middle patch," when doubts typically arise. He pointed me to St Paul's view "for God's gifts and his call are irrevocable" (Romans 11:29). He also reminded me that the church was abundantly endowed with preachers but had very few bankers.

At about the same time, I decided to fast and pray about my future. I was still wondering whether I should stay in finance. I had reflected, analyzed, talked to my wife and close friends. I went for a walk along the Thames and decided to read the last chapter of Luke and the beginning of Acts. As I read, I had an extraordinary sense of release, the fog of uncertainty cleared, and one verse leapt out at me: "Stay in the city until you have been clothed with power from on high" (Luke 24:49). The immediate circumstances to which this verse refers were wholly different from mine, but I had no doubt then, and have no doubt now, that this was God's whispered encouragement for me to stay working in the city of London. I also began to see in a new way that God seeks obedience more than sacrifice. At times, I think the idea of making a sacrifice for God by leaving my career appealed to me but, as I read Acts 5:32, I realized that God gives the Holy Spirit not purely inspirationally, but to those who obey him. I had assumed that the time had come when I would be filled with the Spirit or a new ministry and would leave the city. I was mistaken. In the years thereafter it has become clear that God gives us the power of the Spirit to equip us both for day-to-day work and, if he calls us to it, a wider ministry.

TWIN TRACK—SUCCESS AND SIGNIFICANCE

As part of the struggle to balance our lives, many people decide to change their lifestyle and move to less stressful jobs. These down-shifting moves offer greater opportunities for leisure, but they are not a cure-all and often do not add that key dimension to a successful working life: not just more leisure, but significance. Most of us would like to experience the satisfaction of being involved with people who make change happen. We often look at our lives—usually at the lowest point—and then compare it to some specially significant vocational calling. Significance is not something achieved late in life after giving up a full-time job. Our aim is to be significant at every stage of our working lives. Jean-Pierre Garnier, the former chief executive of a large pharmaceutical company, put it this way: "Being successful means success in everything. If you look for only one dimension in your life, you'll be sad when it stops and there is nothing else."[3] We want to be "happening people."

I found the twin-track option to be one of the best ways of dealing with this issue for those in full-time work: one track is a fulfilled working life and the other is a complementary, probably charitable, activity. We may be able to use skills honed in the workplace for altruistic purposes, or find ways to exploit talents that would otherwise remain unused. I found it hugely encouraging to have a purpose-led job but also to chair Alpha International, whose vision is to spread the Christian good news. Remembering what God has done for me makes me want to share it with others. However, I have never had the time, skill, or calling to be a full-time evangelist. Chairing Alpha International enables me to play a role and share in the excitement. I chose Alpha International: first, because I was asked by a close friend, Nicky Gumbel, who pioneered the Alpha Course; second, because it reflects my own passions; and third, because I am able to contribute to its structures and management. I bring a global perspective, experience of fund-raising and budgets, and management skills, using my expertise in the workplace to the advantage of a voluntary organization. I usually spend a couple of hours a week on Alpha International, plus the occasional evening dinner and board meeting, phone calls, and thinking time at the weekend. This small input of time seems to make a difference. Although I have chosen to work with friends on this, our relationship in this context is professional.

I really enjoy my job working in a busy London hospital as a senior pharmacist. However, I also feel called to prison work. I used to take days off to go on prison visits and to coordinate prayer meetings at my local church for the prisoners whenever I could. I felt increasingly under pressure as I struggled to maintain my commitment to both. I started to consider working a four-day week but felt sure this would not be possible as the department was already short-staffed. To my surprise, my boss agreed to give me Thursdays off. I then discovered that the chaplain at the local prison needed volunteers on a Thursday. This confirmed to me that the decision was right: God was calling me both to pharmacy and to prison work.

—SARAH STOLL, PHARMACIST

HOT-DESKING AND JOB-SHARING—NEW WAYS OF WORKING

The workplace is changing rapidly. Changes range from the desire for smaller networks and supportive teams to new working patterns such as hot-desking, flexi-hours, job-sharing, and, increasingly, working remotely or from home. These developments will not be problem-free, but I hope they will enable both men and women to enjoy being with their children more while also having a fulfilling career. For couples starting out, it is important to discuss the timing of children, particularly in relation to their working patterns over the course of their life together. In some cases, one will be the breadwinner and the other will run the home, whereas others will choose a more flexible working arrangement. Whatever pattern we follow, we need to learn how to take advantage of changes in the workplace to facilitate our callings. One option is portfolio working, where one person takes on several different part-time jobs or roles, thus building up their own unique career portfolio. But we need to take care that these different activities do not lead us into a short-term mentality.

I worked on a charitable project with Nick Turner, who used to have a full-time media consultancy job but left to become a portfolio worker. I asked him for a practical glimpse at his new working week.

> For the last three years I have been, so I am reliably informed, a portfolio worker. I have my own media company, run an Internet project for a charity, head up the art and media ministry for a church, and spend a day a week at art college.

This seems to fit the stage of career I am now at and is made possible by structured training and skills development in the past and a belief that anything is possible.

A typical working week consists of fixed days and flexible days—the fixed days are for the jobs or projects that require regular interaction with others and some rigidity of structure. An example of that would be working every Thursday at church—everyone knows I will be there and available, so meetings and work can be booked in regularly. Another fixed day is the day I spend at art college. The flexible days are the days I spend either doing any freelance work for my media company, fitting in my own art studio time, or completing the regular but less urgent tasks that are involved with running the Internet project.

A typical week looks like this:

Monday—flexible time, mix of admin, project, and freelance work

Tuesday—art studio time (if possible!)

Wednesday—flexible time, mix of admin, project, and freelance work

Thursday—church

Friday—art college

Saturday—hopefully free!

Sunday—free, though I am sometimes involved in church services

This way of living my life has advantages and disadvantages. On the plus side life is never dull and every day is different. However, I have found that time management is a big issue, particularly when something goes wrong in one part of my portfolio, whether a business deadline, an unfinished painting, or an angry e-mail requiring a response. To stop myself going mad I have had to be very disciplined with my time and have also had to make clear to my clients, bosses, and colleagues that I will not necessarily be able to respond to all calls and e-mails immediately (unless urgent). This is probably the biggest pressure I face.

I definitely earn less than when I worked full-time for one organization, because some of my time is spent on my (unpaid) art and charity work. I could not have afforded to work like this in my early years in London and may not always be able to in the future. If we have a family, my wife and I will need to reassess our working patterns and joint income together. I do feel that it has been good for me to step out of the trap of earning as much money as possible, which was incredibly alluring for a while. It is interesting how much money can be saved when you start budgeting, without particularly noticing any change in lifestyle!

Even if the mix of jobs and roles seems haphazard to an outsider, I think there needs to be some cohesion to the portfolio. This could be to develop complementary skills, to combine stressful and stress-releasing roles, or to fund one part of your life with earnings from another, but the key is to know why you are doing it. I love stressful projects and roles, but only in moderation. I have found painting to be the most stress-releasing activity for me.

By enrolling at art college and thus forcing stress-releasing elements into my routine, I have been able to enjoy the stressful times more and also feel more balanced as a person.

My main aim at the moment is to explore areas of my gifts, skills, and personality that I had probably repressed for a number of years—especially fine art and creativity in general. As to how this will develop—I haven't really got a clue, but I want to be open to where God leads me.

—NICK TURNER, PORTFOLIO WORKER

The pressures of modern living, the demands of the workplace, the stress of travel, and the many other personal and financial issues we face each day require us to take seriously a comprehensive review of our lifestyle. Our Maker simply did not wire us to work at full tilt without regard to the enduring priorities of our relationships outside the workplace. Of course, it is true to say that certain jobs are more demanding and require greater levels of stress tolerance than others. And we may well have to say, "It's too hot for me in this kitchen. I'm getting out." Where we do stay, we have to ensure that our priorities reflect God's priorities for our lives. If we weight the scales with our own agenda for achievement, we will never live the hard-working, balanced, and fulfilled lives for which we were made. God is not honored by any way of life that dehumanizes us.

> "WE ARE SIMPLY NOT WIRED BY THE MAKER TO WORK AT FULL TILT WITHOUT REGARD TO THE ENDURING PRIORITIES OF OUR RELATIONSHIPS OUTSIDE THE WORKPLACE."

SIX

STRESS

TWO HUNDRED MEN WERE MONITORED OVER TEN YEARS FOR THE Work Site Blood Pressure Study, published in the *American Journal of Epidemiology*. The study revealed that stress at work puts the same strain on the heart as being forty pounds over-weight, and that prolonged bouts of tension have the same effect on blood pressure as aging thirty years.[1]

Of all the lifestyle issues we face today in the workplace, stress is the most prevalent. It is also a national health problem. Each year, 1.2 million people in the United Kingdom visit their doctors due to workplace stress-related illness.[2] Is it possible to live well in a stressed-out workplace? Is this stress just a fact of modern living? Should we tough it out for as long as possible and then quit? Does faith make a difference?

HARD-PRESSED AND HEMMED IN— WHAT DOES STRESS FEEL LIKE?

We are often tempted to react against the pressure in our lives. In an article in *The Guardian*, psychoanalyst and author Adam Phillips lamented our stressed lives and offered an unusual, if unreal, solution.

> One of the more distracting things about capitalist culture. . .
> is that there is no stupor, no time to vegetate. What I would
> suggest is more time wasting, less stimulation. We need time
> to lie fallow like we did in childhood, so we can recuperate.
> Rather than be constantly told what you want and be pressur-
> ized to go after it, I think we would benefit greatly from spells
> of vaguely restless boredom in which desire can crystallize.[3]

We all know what it feels like to be stressed. It is the point at which others' expectations of us and our ability to deliver fail to match. All around us every day we hear, "I'm stressed out," "I'm really pushed," "I'm out of control," "I'm not coping." Exhaustion and stress go hand in hand. St Paul, writing to the Corinthians, used the image of being "hard pressed on every side" (2 Corinthians 4:8) or, put another way, being squeezed from every side. I know that feeling as part of everyday life: being squeezed like toothpaste through the tube. There are too many demands and not enough time. There's no space to stop and think.

In Mark 4 Jesus told the story of the sower who plants his seed: some of it falls on stony ground, some falls among the thorns, and some in good soil. The seed—the teaching of God—that falls in good soil germinates and produces fruit. I am particularly struck by the image of the seed that falls among thorns, because this is so often what happens to the Christian at work. Here the words are heard and a new lifestyle is adopted, "but the worries of this life, the deceitfulness of wealth and the desires for other things come in and choke the word, making it unfruitful" (v. 19). The Greek word used here for "choke" is a powerful one. It is not merely describing a coughing fit, but a totally overwhelming choking, almost a drowning experience. We can be overwhelmed in many ways: by the big questions— Why am I here? What am I working for? We can be deceived by the promises of material wealth. Or we can simply be stressed by the other things: long hours, unrealistic deadlines, targets, appraisals, paying the mortgage, filling the fridge, keeping up.

At times, stress manifests itself physically: not being able to eat, stomach problems, insomnia, or tightness around the chest. It may also show itself psychologically: we are distracted and unable to concentrate on our work, beset by irrational fears or aggressive to our colleagues. Stress is also spiritual. Above everything else, I have found that it destroys perspective, often making me become self-absorbed. Stress strangles our relationships both with other people and with God, because we cannot lift our heads to see the wider picture. This preoccupation easily becomes obsessive and we lose the ability to think beyond our current fixation. As the parable shows, stress chokes us into low productivity at work.

I normally have the good fortune to sleep extremely well

and have even been known to nod off at the dinner table. If, therefore, I wake preoccupied in the middle of the night, I know that I must be deeply stressed. On one occasion, I was involved with a major securities transaction. Investment banks buy and sell shares as part of their day-to-day business. Often sellers of shares want a fixed price for their shares and invite a bank to purchase these shares before offering them for sale to investors. The risk is then passed to the bank, and the seller has certainty of the proceeds. Until the bank is able to dispose of the shares, it still owns the shares. If the price goes up money is made, and if it goes down losses are incurred. We had just made a difficult pricing decision and I was anxious to see whether the market would prove us right the following morning. I woke in the early hours, tossed and turned, but could not get back to sleep. The critical day had not started, so all I could do was wait. I could not even talk to anyone as it was the middle of the night. Restless anxiety continued to eat away at me. I decided to get up and, somewhat mechanically, read through some psalms to try to obtain a wider perspective. I prayed that our judgment would be vindicated.

The next morning, however, the share price declined. My anxiety thus continued for a few days until, happily in this case, the price recovered and we could sell the shares without loss. This does not always happen. There are times for all of us when we simply have to sweat it out, knowing that God is with us through stressful times even if we don't always get the result we hope for.

Stress is not necessarily the same as pressure. Many of us thrive under pressure but wilt under persistent stress.

Pressure comes from without—and I do not mind pressure. In many ways it gives me a buzz. I would define pressure as being challenged by a project or situation, whether in terms of complexity or timescale or both. I find that it stimulates me and makes the adrenaline flow so that I can accomplish more than seems possible. Stress, which I do not relish, comes from within. To me, stress is the pressure I put on myself internally to meet unrealistic deadlines. This leads to frustration or even a sense of hopelessness about the enormity of the task. I find this very disempowering. While pressure simulates, stress drains and grinds down, and yet is worn by some colleagues as a badge of honor.

—HANNAH REID, CITY LAWYER

JESUS AND STRESS—A WAY THROUGH

Stress is not a modern invention, although its intensity may have increased in our generation. Jesus was no stranger to stress. He knew what it was like to feel hemmed in, but he also knew that he was called to a wider purpose—to see goodness prevail over evil. He was in constant demand as a public figure—a celebrity: people wanted him to be king, and to be available to the crowds. He knew exhaustion and the need to get away. He confronted the merchants in the temple and drove them out when their actions desecrated the place of worship (Mark 11:15–17). He was misunderstood—even by his own disciples—denied by his friend Peter, and betrayed by Judas.

If I find myself pushed and exhausted after traveling a lot, I often draw strength from one stressful day in the life of Jesus recorded in Luke 8:22–56. Jesus and the disciples set out in a boat. He fell asleep, I believe, so exhausted that even a raging storm did not wake him up. He was woken by panicking disciples and he quelled the storm. On setting foot on the opposite shore he exorcised a demon-possessed man, bringing ruin to the local Gadarene farmer whose herd of pigs were taken over by those same demons, causing them to rush into the lake and drown. After that, the fearful people asked him to leave them. Hardly had he returned across the lake than he agreed to Jairus's plea to visit his dying daughter. While en route he was mobbed and his garment touched in faith by a woman with bleeding, whom he healed.

Then Jairus's daughter died. He was told not to bother going to see her, but Jesus nonetheless pressed on. He arrived at Jairus's house and shut up the funeral wailers, saying that she was simply asleep and not dead. They laughed at him but still he raised her from the dead. It is all here: exhaustion, loneliness, traveling, trying to catch up on sleep, interrupted sleep, the demands of friends, the fear of failure, the taunts of the worldly-wise.

When Jesus preached his first sermon in Nazareth, his hometown rejoiced at his remarkable teaching—he was the local boy made good. Luke tells us that "all spoke well of him" (Luke 4:22). But, within the day, the temperature changed as he preached: "All the people in the synagogue were furious when they heard this. They got up, drove him out of the town, and took him to the brow of the hill on which the town was built, in order to throw him down the cliff. But he walked right through the crowd and went on his way" (vv. 28–30). This is a great example for us. When it seemed that everyone had turned against him, Jesus did not run for cover; he walked through the midst of the crowd and went on his way. This is the authority of a person convinced of his calling and of the power of God to help him. Jesus said, "I know where I came from and where I am going" (John 8:14).

We can do what Jesus did. Many times I have turned to this teaching when I have felt the world closing in on me. When we feel overwhelmed by the demands of the workplace, we don't have to outflank the pressure around us. We can, and we must, face it head-on. The Spirit of God empowers us, like Christ, to walk through the midst of our stress.

CHILLED, NOT CHOKED—HOW DO WE DEAL WITH STRESS?

Some stress (for example, that which results in clinical depression) requires medical attention. Stress is not a sign of personal weakness, and we should not be ashamed to ask for help if we are overwhelmed. However, my aim here is to consider stress in everyday work situations. When Jesus comforted his disciples shortly before his death, he started with the perspective of eternity: "In my Father's house are many rooms; if it were not so, I would have told you. I am going there to prepare a place for you. And if I go and prepare a place for you, I will come back and take you to be with me" (John 14:2–3). When we see our lives in the security of this wider context, the things that stress us out can seem much more manageable. Jesus went on to speak about the promised Holy Spirit and said, "Peace I leave with you; my peace I give you. I do not give to you as the world gives. Do not let your hearts be troubled and do not be afraid" (v. 27). We need to root our lives in the peace that Christ has given us if we are to deal effectively with stress. This means nurturing our relationship with God at all times through consistent reading of the Bible, developing intimacy with God, prayer, and the use of other spiritual disciplines.

In Psalm 18, David said, "In my distress [i.e., "When I was under pressure"] I called to the LORD; I cried to my God for help" (v. 6). This call is answered in verse 19: "He brought me out into a spacious place; he rescued me because he delighted in me." These verses have meant more to me in the harshness of the working environment than almost any other psalm. The love of God—his delight in me—transforms my perspective in the workplace. The "spacious place" of verse 19 is what I long for—room to maneuver and a chance to recover God's peace. God is the space giver; the devil is the space invader. I therefore try to look for the God-given spacious place in the midst of stress. Christian stress-busting is not a new self-help technique but an outworking of following Christ. I have tried to follow seven biblical strategies to keep stress in check. I hope they may be helpful to you.

> "WE NEED TO ROOT OUR LIVES IN THE PEACE THAT CHRIST HAS GIVEN US IF WE ARE TO DEAL EFFECTIVELY WITH STRESS."

1. Stay healthy

At its most basic, we need to look after our bodies by taking regular breaks, eating well, and exercising regularly. Our bodies are, after all, temples of the Holy Spirit (1 Corinthians 6:19) and need to be looked after. This is simply common sense, but in times of stress and deadlines, it can be the first thing to go. I remember a time in the middle of a complicated takeover bid by one major UK company of another, when I tried to take a break each day to go to a nearby gym. I could not plan this ahead but grabbed the opportunity whenever it arose. This parity helped to clear my mind, but mostly it relieved the tension of constant decision making. A lawyer told me that, during one seemingly never-ending deal, he often found himself at ten at night checking whether the team had consumed anything other than caffeine that day. Generally they hadn't and he ordered in food for them. He was amazed how much more quickly they got through everything once they had eaten!

2. Fight fear

I remember reading Psalm 112:7 one morning to learn that the people who trust the Lord "will have no fear of bad news; their hearts are steadfast, trusting in the LORD." I was praying I sensed that all was not well at work and that it would be an important day. I had no idea what that meant, but I knew that the Spirit of God was preparing me. The words "will have no fear of bad

> "GOD IS THE SPACE GIVER; THE DEVIL IS THE SPACE INVADER."

news" repeated themselves in my head throughout the day. At the end of the day I was called into the chairman's office. He told me that one of my best clients had decided that I was not the right person to advise him. In normal circumstances I would have been devastated. Of course I felt gutted, but the day's preparation meant that I was ready to receive the news. I did not need to fear bad news. This did not mean that there wasn't any but that I did not need to fear it. This assurance enabled me to come through a difficult time with confidence. The client wrote me a very gracious letter explaining his reasons; I knew he was right. I spoke to him and was able to accept his judgment without rancor. I did not feel the need to rerun history or to justify my actions, which would have been my natural reaction. I then felt a curious freedom in handing over the account to a colleague. I was able to offer help behind the scenes with genuine willingness. I had, after all, received the tip-off!

> "IT IS VALUABLE TO BUILD UP A RESERVOIR OF THE SPECIFIC WAYS IN WHICH GOD HAS HELPED US IN THE PAST TO REMIND US THAT GOD IS REAL AND THAT HE IS GOOD."

3. Take joy seriously

In 1 Thessalonians, Paul wrote, "Be joyful always" (5:16). In times of stress we particularly need to look around us and focus consciously on what lifts our spirits. When you are streaming out of a crowded subway station, or stuck in traffic, or having to stand on a crowded bus, or queuing to get through a congested immigration line, take time to notice a bird in a tree or a beautiful piece of architecture. I remember rushing out of a meeting and seeing an elderly couple holding hands and chatting as they walked down the street together. This boosted my day, reminding me of enduring values beyond the day-to-day stress. Small things can make a big difference to our mood. It is valuable to build up a reservoir of the specific ways in which God has helped us in the past to remind us that God is real and that he is good.

4. Take an emotional break

Nobody functions well in prolonged periods of unremitting stress. If I feel I am losing my sense of perspective, I often make a phone call to a friend or write an e-mail or tweet that has nothing to do with work. I find it restores my sense of humanity to connect with people in different situations from my own. Even if they are also stressed, just talking together takes me out of the cocoon of my own preoccupations. In times of stress, my wife, Fi, and I have to work out what is the best way of spending time together. If I am particularly tired, a dinner for two can become an action replay of my stressful day. If both of us are under pressure, the temptation can be to compete about how bad things have been. A trip to the theatre or cinema can enable us to enjoy being together without increasing our stress levels. Sometimes it helps, if both of us agree, not to talk about a particularly pressing issue but instead to try to enjoy simply being together.

In times of high stress, I often feel desperate for a time of song worship. I long for the times of worship on Sunday or try to meet with a few others to worship. Worshipping together helps me maintain the intimacy of my relationship with God, which stress can so easily erode.

5. Minister in the opposite spirit

Paul said, "We work hard with our own hands. When we are cursed, we bless; when we are persecuted, we endure it; when we are slandered, we answer kindly" (1 Corinthians 4:12–13). When a colleague trashes our work, we shouldn't snap back but instead commend them on a piece of their work. And when others criticize us, we should aim to answer gently. This is easy to agree with but very hard to do. I try to change gears by asking for help from the Spirit of God—and only then do I speak. This is the spiritual equivalent of counting to ten. But so often I fail—and lash out. I then feel dreadful. Ministering in the opposite spirit is usually a painful process.

After only a few days in my new job at the hospital, I seemed to keep having altercations with one of the reception staff. She would respond to my polite civilities with what appeared to be complaint after complaint. She would claim that my handwriting wasn't clear enough (this from a woman who works with doctors!) and object to my clinic list being handed in a few minutes late. I assumed that it was because I was a lowly physiotherapist and not a terribly grand consultant that she treated me with such disdain.

Several weeks later I had to cancel a clinic at short notice and so left word with the reception staff. When I returned there was a barrage of complaints from patients who had traveled to the hospital before being informed that the clinic was canceled. These complaints finally gave me the impetus I needed to confront the issues. Despite a creeping feeling that I was being bullied by someone in a less senior position, I chose a quiet moment and sat down with the receptionist. I decided not to pull rank but rather to ask whether I had offended her and why she hadn't cancelled my patients. After the inevitable momentary defensiveness, it turned out she had assumed that I had my own secretarial support and that the clinic patients were my sole responsibility. Our mistaken assumptions about each other's roles and attitudes proved to be the only stumbling block to working out a solution.

Several months later, she took the time to come to me and, much to her credit, apologized. On reflection I was so pleased that I had not reacted in a retaliatory manner, as this would have compounded the difficulties of both our situations.

—ANITA PATEL, PHYSIOTHERAPIST

6. Take control of our thoughts

In my experience, in times of high anxiety the prevailing wind is negativity and thoughts can easily spiral downward. A persistent questioning can arise from the depths of the inner self relating to fear of the future, what others think of us, or whether there is any significance in what we are doing. When this happens, the first thing I try to do is reject the thoughts that are without substance. I then remind myself of one of the many attributes of God—for example, his love—and then dwell on it. Paul wrote, "whatever is true, whatever is noble, whatever is right, whatever is pure, whatever is lovely, whatever is admirable—if anything is excellent or praiseworthy—think about such things" (Philippians 4:8). The mind is a gateway, which we control. With God's help we can choose to open it to good and close it to fear, uncertainty, and self-righteousness. In *Paradise Lost*, the poet John Milton captured this thought: "The mind is its own place, and in itself can make a heaven of hell, a hell of heaven."⁴ It is within our control to regulate what we dwell on: the discipline of breaking a negative spiral is a key weapon in our desire to eliminate stress.

One way of breaking the drag of negative thoughts is to go on a "starvation diet." Set a time—say, one full day—and deliberately try to starve yourself of any negative thoughts. At the same time allow space for the Spirit of God to engage your mind with the good, the wholesome, and the positive aspects of life and meditate on these.

A business development manager told me that in times of stress he tries to find a quiet place and speak his concerns aloud. He also keeps a pad of paper next to his bed to write down thoughts that preoccupy him and prevent him from sleeping. These techniques stop his anxieties from dominating his thought life and leave him free to move on.

Different strategies work for different people. Steve, a print worker, found it helpful to set aside a "worry time." He told me that, while running his business, he went through a terrible experience and was frantic with anxiety about a certain issue. A friend advised him to set aside a time of day to worry about it, for example, between 9:00 A.M. and 9:15 A.M. This technique helped keep him sane. If a letter or e-mail came through about the issue, he would just leave it in the inbox and read it during his "worry time." If there was a phone call, he said that he was busy and arranged to call back during the worry time! If he woke up in the middle of the night in a panic, he would say to himself, "No, I am not thinking about this now. I will think about it tomorrow at 9:00 A.M." He found that, when he did this, it shrank the problem and made it manageable. Life could carry on outside the worry time, and it stopped him being anxious all the time and having endless circular conversations with his wife.

I have also found it helpful to break time into manageable sections, sometimes aiming just to get through the morning until lunchtime. It is important to set a future point to look forward to, for example, deciding to watch Manchester United play soccer next Wednesday or meeting friends for dinner at the end of the week. This can help counter the feeling that there is no end in sight. When huge problems seem to be hovering on the horizon, I try to remember Jesus' words: "Therefore do not worry about tomorrow, for tomorrow will worry about itself. Each day has enough trouble of its own" (Matthew 6:34). When stress is high we should live in a world of contracting horizons.

7. Pray and read the Bible

For me, the most important way to gain perspective in times of stress is through prayer, remembering of course that the primary objective of prayer is to bring glory to God, and not to beat stress. Paul wrote in Philippians, "Do not be anxious about anything, but in everything, by prayer and petition, with thanksgiving, present your requests to God" (4:6). In the past I have attended extremely tense meetings where the parties have been at loggerheads with each other. I try to turn to God and to pray silently. The acrimony often, but by no means invariably, seems to disappear. I cannot prove the causality, but it seems to happen more often when I pray.

Intercession on the run is not sufficient but can be helpful. Most of my petitionary prayer happens when I am traveling. I know many people who pray whenever going to a fixed point in the office—the lift, the coffee machine, or photocopier. We also need to set patterns of prayer. Monday morning is a good time to prepare spiritually for the week ahead. As the week starts, I like to remind myself that there is a spiritual "can-do" aspect to work, however stressful the week may turn out to be. I think of Numbers 13:30, when God had told the Israelites to explore the land of Canaan, which he was giving to them. On their return the majority were afraid and pessimistic about their ability to take the land. Caleb had a different attitude and said, "We should go up and take possession of the land, for we can certainly do it." When God is with us he equips us for the task at hand, even if it appears over-whelming. On weekday mornings I try to pray and read at least the New Testament section of my *Bible in One Year*[5] before I get to work. I consider the weekends "catch-up time", a chance to build up spiritual capital, which can run down quickly during the week.

I was quite struck by the testimony of the power of prayer recounted by a former colleague of mine who left the company where we worked together, to set up his own business.

I miscalculated quite severely how long it would take to get a consulting business of this kind to break even. Like most entrepreneurs, I had taken out a mortgage on the house to provide us with enough money to live for eighteen months while we got it going. I had neglected to foresee a swift and dramatic business downturn. So we were left with cash resources dwindling and not much in the way of business prospects. During this period, I started feeling massively stressed, upset, and on the verge of tears on a regular basis. I had never before been without money, and it was a very unfamiliar experience. My wife and I had cut back expenses pretty hard, but we were still spending more than I was able to earn. I felt embarrassed talking to my friends, who would inevitably ask how it was going. I tried to be cheerful, but it was inauthentic.

I started praying like never before, reading the Bible each morning at 6:00 or 6:30, the overall structure provided by the Lord's Prayer. I did not ask for too much in the way of money, but rather that I would be filled with peace and would do the kind of work God wanted me to do. I began to pray for guidance, wisdom, and discernment. I also started praying a lot for others, the church, and friends, and attempted to be thankful for what I had. Sometimes an hour would go by and I wouldn't even notice.

The effect of this praying was quite amazing. When I was really going through the stressful patch, I would not stop praying until I felt filled with the Spirit. I don't know how to define that except to say I felt confident and relaxed during each day that things were going to turn out okay. Here I

113

was, an entrepreneur running out of money, in the middle of a terrible recession, realizing that he does not really have a clue what he is doing or what his product is, and yet feeling quite relaxed about it. People started telling me how well I looked, younger and healthier. I could not get over this at all. I can honestly say I went through the hardest time of my life professionally, and felt younger at the end of it!

I also started to develop real compassion for people who have to struggle with money every month, and I could see how debilitating money worries can be, especially if one has a family to provide for. It has been a very humbling experience for a former arrogant and successful banker. God taught me a valuable lesson. I determined that, when the money started flowing, we would give away what we did not need, rather than hoarding it for a "rainy day" or for "financial independence." It has really changed my values. I would not have traded this experience for the world.

—MILES PROTTER, MANAGING
PARTNER OF THE VALUES PARTNERSHIP

Prayer is the vital oxygen for living. It is simply not possible to function without these regular times of hearing and then recalibrating our ways accordingly. We need to understand our own temperament and then to find a prayer routine that suits us, including Bible reading, reflecting, singing, and meditating. Eugene Peterson, the writer and Bible translator, talks of the Bible as "everyday robust sanity."[6] We need this reality check, which comes from reading the Bible, to destress our lives. The most liberating moment comes when we realize that there is no one-size-fits-all prayer methodology. We all need to pray, but the way in which we do so should reflect the rich variety of God's ways of speaking to us. One way I find most powerful is the prayer of praise. Praise is our weapon of first resort. We can live under pressure if our perspective of God is right. Our understanding of the greatness of God leads us to despair of our own strength and to turn to God, the only one who can make sense of the complex world he has created. Praise is the war cry of the Christian asserting God's supremacy over the whole of life, including the workplace. I believe that nothing breaks the self-centeredness of a centered life as much as the words "I praise you, Lord."

During the Battle of Trafalgar two-hundredth-anniversary celebrations in 2005, I became fascinated by the life of Lord Nelson. Twice daily, all his life, he studied and recorded the weather—what the wind, waves, swell, and temperature were doing. He did so whether on land or on sea. It must have been the most dull routine! Yet, in the moment of critical judgment at the Battle of Trafalgar, Nelson drew on this reservoir of knowledge and insight as he observed that a change in the swell of the sea pointed to an advancing storm days before it broke. Instead of having a conventional debate where the two lines of ships lined up against each other in parallel, he seized the advantage offered by the sea to slice through and destroy the combined armada. His daily habit gave him the experience and confidence to make that decisive judgment at a critical time in Britain's history.

We never know when the storms of life will hit us. We

therefore need to build up our memory bank and to be prepared. One way of doing so is to develop the daily habit of regular prayer. We will then be in much better shape to face the unexpected stress when it comes.

SEVEN

FAILURE, DISAPPOINTMENT, AND HOPE

EVERYONE EXPERIENCES FAILURE AND DISAPPOINTMENT. IT OFTEN starts early in life and the memories, oftentimes trivial, stay with us, and sometimes shape our decisions even decades later. When I was about sixteen, I was chairman of the school debating society. A major debate about the apartheid system was organized, and I prepared myself to speak passionately against it. I felt that the righteousness of our cause would easily win. However, we lost. I realized that I had not taken into account the forces of naked prejudice.

This failure to persuade a group of my peers of such obvious injustice has never left me, and even now I prefer not to think about the pain of what seemed to me a deeply personal rejection. Objectively, it was a passing moment of little consequence, but it has stayed with me. In our working lives it is unusual not to experience disappointment. We are overlooked for promotion or made redundant; a crucial deal folds or we fail to secure an agent; a team member betrays us or lets us down, or we make a mistake that fills us with shame. And what is shame but that which, when recalled to our conscious mind, we wish were not there? In these situations, how is it possible to find hope, deal with failure and disappointment, and find a spur to drive us on beyond the gloom?

FAITH AND ETERNITY—THE BASIS OF CHRISTIAN HOPE

In difficult times, I have often tried to learn from Paul's example. He knew where the source of his strength came from: "To this end I labor, struggling with all [God's] energy, which so powerfully works in me" (Colossians 1:29). The energy for living well comes from a source outside of us yet works to change us from within. The source of Christian hope arises from the knowledge that we are made by a God who loves each one of us. We have renewed a relationship with him through the life, death, and resurrection of Jesus. We look forward to his return. It is this cosmic context that provides the framework for our everyday lives. In a fast-moving world, I think it is essential that we fix our minds and hearts on the hope that Christ has given us, and then we move the other pieces around this.

Christian hope is not mere optimism or a projection of our desires. It is not the same as saying, "I hope it doesn't rain."

Paul wrote that "hope does not disappoint us, because God has poured out his love into our hearts by the Holy Spirit, whom he has given us" (Romans 5:5). Jesus inaugurated the kingdom of God when he came to earth, and he won the decisive victory over evil and disappointment on the cross. As we work in partnership with God, drawing his values into the world, we are called to lay down our lives, identifying with Jesus on the cross and sharing in the same resurrection power. Paul used rich commercial words to describe this relationship. He wrote: "He anointed us, set his seal of ownership on us, and put his Spirit in our hearts as a deposit, guaranteeing what is to come" (2 Corinthians 1:21–22). The same word Paul used for "anointed" is also the word used for "investd in." God has invested in our lives, marking us with an outward sign (seal) of his ownership. The Holy Spirit is a "deposit" guaranteeing now the full payment later.

Thus we are utterly secure in this life because Christ has underwritten his investment in us. Our lives, therefore, have eternal value.

I remember my student days in South Africa, at a very dark time in the country's history. We used to crouch over the radio, listening to the BBC World Service. My friends and I were passionate about abolishing apartheid and establishing justice, and it gave us such hope for our own work to hear from the regular broadcasts that there was another world where people lived by decent values. We all need some experience outside ourselves to cling to when our hope is under pressure. The Christian is sustained by the knowledge that this world is not all there is.

THE GREAT EXCHANGE—HOW
DO WE DEAL WITH OUR MISTAKES?

"WE ALL NEED SOME EXPERIENCE OUTSIDE OURSELVES TO CLING TO WHEN OUR HOPE IS UNDER PRESSURE."

Dominating the city of London is a magnificent building called the Royal Exchange, where major commercial transactions were once carried out. As I walked past the building one morning, I suddenly saw in my mind's eye an image of what Christ did on the cross for us. It was a royal exchange. Exchange is the image of the marketplace. Financial traders talk about convertible bonds and interest rate swaps, and all of us have paged through *Exchange and Mart* and understand the concept of bartering goods. Every day we can ask God to take our guilt, mistakes, and failures and exchange them for peace, security, and purpose. We enter into the trade simply by asking him to take the acts and omissions that cause displeasure to him—our sin. This is as real a transaction as anyone buying, for example, a car: you take your money, you give it to the dealer, and he exchanges it for a vehicle. But there is a difference. We bring nothing. Jesus gives us a trade that we do not deserve, and completes the bargain as if he were on both sides. Imagine someone going into a bureau de change with a stack of retired currency—French francs or German marks. They would of course be rejected, because they would be bringing nothing to the trade. French francs cannot be exchanged for

US dollars—they are worthless; they ceased to have any value with the creation of the euro. Imagine if someone were prepared to accept the trade. We would think them either astonishingly stupid or amazingly generous. Why would someone exchange valuable assets for worthlessness? But this is precisely what Jesus did on the cross. He entered into the Great Exchange, by which he gave us his riches for our poverty. "For you know the grace of our Lord Jesus Christ, that though he was rich, yet for your sakes he became poor, so that you through his poverty might become rich" (2 Corinthians 8:9). This is a compelling verse: riches for poverty, life for death, freedom for guilt.

ONGOING FORGIVENESS—HOW CAN WE RESTORE RELATIONSHIP?

To maintain good relationships, we need to learn to say sorry and to practice forgiveness in the workplace. You may say, "Forgiveness is fine at church, but surely not at work, right?"

But, as Christians, we know that we are forgiven sinners and this enables us to take the lead. I find that, when I have been working under demanding conditions, particularly if I am overly tired, I need to be especially vigilant about my reactions to people. This is a subject that Jesus spoke about on more than one occasion—probably because he knew how difficult we would find it. It forms part of the Lord's Prayer, and is actually the only part of the prayer that is then immediately elaborated upon, underlining its importance (Matthew 6:9–15).

Whenever we feel we have stepped out of line, I think we need to apologize. Similarly, if we feel we have been wronged, it is constructive to approach the other person only after a short interval (of perhaps twenty-four to forty-eight hours), to allow our emotions to cool down. We need to work toward an attitude of grace, taking minor issues in our stride.

> I work for rather difficult characters—brilliant in their way but not gifted in managing people. I can find myself building up a list of resentments against them. I have to stop myself and make the effort to pray for them, however little I feel like it, and forgive them for the irritations and injustices I feel I have had to put up with. This always helps me to see them as real people with their own pressures, and improves the working relationship.
>
> —IAN LLOYD, SOLICITOR

One of the great difficulties in the world today is truth decay—many treat truth as a tradable commodity, buying into it only if the return looks promising. It is not just that we should be able to trust particular individuals to tell the truth, but that trustworthy behavior should start to infuse organizations, so that integrity is once again seen as a value to aspire to. Without trust and integrity the free market is endangered. When I attended a World Economic Forum in Davos, Switzerland, "Tough Trust" was the topic for discussion. I thought it was an arresting idea. It is tough to rely on others but we need to do so. We need each other, however much we prefer to go it alone. This trusting interdependence is drawn from the Trinity—Father, Son, and Holy Spirit working together in harmony, collaboration, and complete trust. God is reflected in these endeavors precisely because this is what happens in the eternal Godhead. Could there be a greater model of tough trust than Jesus working with his disciples in a trusting relationship, with all the well-documented strain and joy that this entailed?

But how, practically, do we build trust again once it has been fractured? All of us have deep memories of broken relationships at work. Your idea is taken by someone and passed off as his or her own; someone lies to you about your performance at work, or you are let down without excuse at the last moment on a crucial project. At some time or another we say to ourselves—or to others—"I can't trust Nicola or John again." Yet we know in reality that we have to put aside our differences in order to work together.

On one occasion, a colleague was not straight with me and I subsequently found out from others about his bad-mouthing me. I was furious. Half of me wanted nothing more to do with him; the other half knew we had to work together under one roof and, therefore, had to talk. To be honest, I never wanted to trust him again. But we are created in God's image. The certainties and ferocity of self-righteous outpourings when we are hurt bend to the persistent but much more tentative proddings of conscience. In these circumstances we should take the first step, even if we do so gingerly. After all, it's a very raw nerve that is touched. There is nothing wrong with being wary—but wariness should not replace the willingness to build a new relationship. Reconciliation is at the heart of faith, and this pushes us, usually against our natural instincts, to begin to rebuild trust. And God, who is trustworthy, teaches us to trust again.

But how do we start to put things right? Step one is the desire to set matters straight. Here, too, we know that God inclines our hearts toward reconciliation so that, even if we do not feel inclined to make peace, we can ask him to give us the grace to do so. Thereafter an approach needs to be made. In my case this was a short handwritten letter—e-mail is too often the vehicle for quick rage. Then there should be a frank discussion. There is no lasting value in not being up front about the facts. Expect a response—even a vigorous one. After all, the accusations that one makes regarding a break in trust go to the essence of any person's self-esteem. After the meeting there will not be an automatic reset to the status quo ante. That takes time, but our behavior has to reflect the reality that we have totally forgiven that person. I hope that I did so and that he knew that no grudges were kept.

The Lord's Prayer is invaluable for this reason: "Forgive us our sins as we forgive those who have sinned against us." We forgive as we have been forgiven. We say this prayer not nearly enough. It is truly the manifesto of the person at work. Thus invoked, an energy that comes from outside our own being enables us to walk in the freedom of new trust. Yes, there will be an accusation of naïveté. After all, "Don't trust others" is a slogan for many who have been hurt at work. Sometimes we have to live with the consequences of trusting too readily. That could be part of our calling to suffer with Christ.

Jesus longed for the trust of those around him. He took the

risk of trusting his disciples. All trust involves risk. Jesus was badly let down and betrayed by his disciples—they slept instead of keeping watch (Matthew 26:40), Peter denied all knowledge of him (Matthew 26:69–75), and Judas ultimately betrayed him into the hands of those who would kill him (Luke 22:48). Yet forgiveness and restoration lay at the heart of his message. The drive to trust again arises not out of the need of the workplace but from the very nature of God. Every fractured trust impairs our humanity. Every forgiven breach strengthens it. That's God's way in the world.

FAILURE AND DISAPPOINTMENT— AN OPPORTUNITY TO GROW

It is inevitable that some projects we are involved in will fail, but it is not true that we are failures. I remember a young banker telling me, "I am a failure." This is a devastating statement that may have deadly psychological consequences. It is more accurate to say "I have failed in this project." This enables us to face the reality of the situation without condemning our whole life and person to failure.

Then we need to deal with the chain of negative emotions that can be set off by a perceived failure. Failure is like a train that pulls behind it a coach of disappointment, and linked to that a coach of self-pity, followed by a coach of rejection, a coach of "I've had enough," and finally a coach of all-pervading pessimism. I try not to let my sense of disappointment about a particular failure spread to other areas of my life. I remember working intensely for several months putting together a takeover bid, which was rejected. I was left with an empty diary and no adrenaline, wondering what could have been done better. I went home feeling low and lacking the resilience to cope with minor irritations. On these occasions, I find that what helps me most is to remind myself that God is so much bigger than an adverse decision or a failed transaction. Reading the psalms aloud and alone brings a perspective of the greatness and power of God. Restoring our perspective keeps our feelings of disappointment in their proper place. We are failures only if Christ fails in us, and that he will never do. We can be confident that he who began a good work in us will carry it through to completion (Philippians 1:6).

> "WE ARE FAILURES ONLY IF CHRIST FAILS IN US, AND THAT HE WILL NEVER DO. WE CAN BE CONFIDENT THAT HE WHO BEGAN A GOOD WORK IN US WILL CARRY IT THROUGH TO COMPLETION."

In our achievement-oriented culture, we tend to feel ashamed of our failures. We view them as wholly negative and try to cover them up. But the way we grow is not by pretending that all is well, but by facing disappointment head-on, acknowledging the facts. When the disciples had been working all night and were asked whether they had caught any fish, they must have been tempted to justify their failure. Instead they said, "We have no fish." But they still believed in Jesus' ability to turn their situation around. When they followed his instruction to fish on the right side, their nets were filled to bursting (John 21:6). Similarly, we need to be brutally honest about our failures and to be open to God's guidance, especially in times of crushing disappointment. Constructive criticism helps us learn from our mistakes and is one of the main ways in which we can improve and grow.

As a young trainee, I was working on the first privatization issue for the UK government—the sale of BP shares. I had to prepare a crucial share exchange document that would enable the shares to be distributed from the government to millions of new investors. I messed it up. There was a group of people around my desk waiting. Stress was high and a deadline was approaching. The chairman of the bank was also there and was quite entitled to go ballistic. Instead, he gave the others a new task and, when alone with me, ticked me off (quite rightly), and then showed me how to sort out the vital document. That day I learned a lot about share exchanges, but perhaps more about learning from mistakes.

Failures help to kill our pride and develop humility. This is crucial if we want to follow Jesus and develop a godly character. God promises to work in all things for the good of those who love him (Romans 8:28). This does not mean that he inflicts failure on us, but it does mean that he can use it. He brings good out of bad situations in the most unexpected ways—even when we can't possibly imagine how this might happen. This is illustrated in the life of Joseph, who was sold into slavery by his brothers, abused and imprisoned, but was finally reinstated as the first and only Israelite to become prime minister of Egypt. After all of this, Joseph was able to tell his brothers, "You intended to harm me, but God intended it for good" (Genesis 50:20). Self-employed Roger Philip explains how the effects of perceived failures resulted in an improved outlook on life:

> We went through a three-year period where virtually everything seemed to be going wrong. I lost my job and as a result we got behind on our mortgage repayments. We made a conscious decision not to hide our situation from those who asked, even when they expected a cheery "Christian" answer. At times we felt very vulnerable, particularly when God seemed absent. We realized that we had always assumed that things would work out more or less as we wanted in the end. We have learned to loosen our grip on the future, and on good days feel excitement about where God might lead us. We also live more fully in the present and generally worry less. We have also noticed that our openness about what we've been going through seems to have helped other people to be honest with us about their own hidden struggles, leading to a new depth of relationship.
>
> —ROGER, FOUNDER OF A RECRUITMENT COMPANY

RECOVERING FROM DISAPPOINTMENT— FIVE STEPS TO RENEW OUR HOPE

Laurence van der Post, the South African philosopher and anthropologist who spent his life observing the social patterns of contemporary society and of the nomadic San people in South Africa, remarked, "The lesson of history for me is that men and their societies can endure and surmount any enormities except a state of meaninglessness."[1]

Living each day at work with hope and purpose is essential for our well-being. It is true that those who are purpose-led have a positive outlook on life and produce better results both at work and outside it, influencing the communities in which they live. So it is important to recover hope when, through failure and disappointment, we have lost its power to keep us expectant. How do we do it? Here are five pointers that I have found helpful when trying to recover from disappointment.

1. Turn to God

Following Jesus' crucifixion, two of the disciples were walking to Emmaus, a village about seven miles from Jerusalem. As they discussed recent events, somebody came and joined them and, finding them downcast, inquired what they were talking about. It was only later that they realized the man was Jesus. Initially, they were so preoccupied with their disappointment that they failed to recognize that the Lord of hope was walking alongside them. It is important to face our disappointments honestly and to acknowledge how they make us feel. However, if we do not keep disappointment in its place, it can overwhelm us, and we too risk forgetting that the Lord of hope walks with us through good and bad, and has promised never to abandon us (Matthew 28:20).

When we are down, we often instinctively want to turn away from God, in some way implicating him in our misfortune. This is a great mistake. If we follow the self-help theories, we will dig inside ourselves only to find that there is nothing there to pick us up. We need to take the initiative to lift our heads toward God. As we do so, we are reminded of his love for us, his victory on the cross, and the power of the resurrection. There is a "tensed waiting" on earth as we live in the hope created by the resurrection, which has not yet been fulfilled. Not only is work imperfect, but creation as a whole groans in imperfection, waiting for the new heaven and the new earth promised by God. The hope of Christ's return enables us to live expectantly, even if our present circumstances at work are harsh and negative.

> "IF WE DO NOT KEEP DISAPPOINTMENT IN ITS PLACE, IT CAN OVERWHELM US, AND WE TOO RISK FORGETTING THAT THE LORD OF HOPE WALKS WITH US THROUGH GOOD AND BAD, AND HAS PROMISED NEVER TO ABANDON US."

2. Face the facts

Realism is vital when we come to deal with our disappointments. I find enormous encouragement from Paul's description of Abraham in Romans 4:19–20: "Without weakening in his faith. . . faced the fact that his body was as good as dead—since he was about a hundred years old—and that Sarah's womb was also dead. Yet he did not waver through unbelief regarding the promise of God." Abraham faced the facts that both he and his wife were past childbearing age, yet remained open to God's power to give them a child.

The facts are a radical reality. We need to avoid fantasies and daydreams of what might have been when we deal with our own discouragements: there is no value in an indulgent reconstruction of the past. It is God alone who can change our situation, enabling us to stop dwelling in the past so that he can transform and empower our future.

3. Meditate on Scripture

Led by the Spirit, we find a promise of God in the Bible appropriate to our situation. We then read it, mull it over, and say it aloud until we digest its meaning and its truth becomes part of our being. I find it helpful to memorize and meditate upon particular verses, because hope is so often attacked by negativity and fear. I have committed to memory Romans 15:13, "May the God of hope fill you with all joy and peace as you trust in him, so that you may overflow with hope by the power of the Holy Spirit." By his creative Holy Spirit, God enables us to grow in hope, breaking the bounds of our own insularity and transforming areas of our lives that we have constructed in the belief that God cannot really make a difference.

4. Keep a journal

I normally find it easier to talk than to write but, if I am going through a particularly difficult time, I find it helpful to keep a journal. This enables me to articulate what I am thinking and feeling. Written words seem to have a more objective ring to them—and can also be reviewed at a later date. As I review past disappointments, I can often see God's hand at work,

> "IT IS GOD ALONE WHO CAN CHANGE OUR SITUATION, ENABLING US TO STOP DWELLING IN THE PAST SO THAT HE CAN TRANSFORM AND EMPOWER OUR FUTURE."

bringing good out of situations that seemed hopeless at the time. In retrospect, I can recognize that God gave me "eternal encouragement and good hope" (2 Thessalonians 2:16). The focus of my recollection is changed from "yet another failure" to the good that came out of a time of rejection and disillusionment.

5. Persevere in hope

We naturally long for instant gratification and for a sudden change of mood when we are burdened and feeling a loss of hope in our lives. This is seldom what happens. Character is developed by learning to live through disappointment and recovering hope for the long term. We are not promised that at the end of each day there will be a reversal of the weights that have dragged us down. But we are encouraged that, if we persevere, God will enable us to keep going when we are ready to pack it all in.

Once, at a U2 concert, Bono, the lead singer of the band, recalled his father's advice to him as a young man starting out on a career: "Don't dream. To dream is to be disappointed."[2] Fortunately, Bono did not take this advice. He dared to dream and he risked disappointment. Even if we face disillusionment when our dreams fade or fail, we can emerge from it because Christian hope is dynamic and powerful, whereas disappointment tends to constrict us, reducing our motivation and contracting our horizons. Christian hope expresses abundance, abandonment, creativity, and an openness to renewal.

A client once said to me, "You can either be a pussycat or a tiger in this deal. Now go and be a tiger." Christian hope has too often been domesticated as if it were a pussycat, a good feeling, or a good cause—something to keep us going. We need to recover the tiger—a wild hope.

THE UNFORCED RHYTHMS OF GRACE—
HOW TO LIVE WITH HOPE

When we are down we tend to live dysfunctional lives. It is as if there is a constant sore that we cannot get rid of and which reminds us of the negative tow in our lives. The disciples were often brought down, as we are, by being tired or worn out, and Jesus promised them that he would restore a new rhythm to their lives and would show them how to live freely and lightly. Life has a rhythm for each one of us that is given to us by God to enable us to live each day in sync with his grace and love. Our task is to seek his will and then to align our lives with his purposes. This will inevitably involve a close scrutiny of our patterns of living, our workload in the office, and the other activities that frequently disrupt our well-being and motivation. We may well have to cut out activities that are fruitless and cause us to be exhausted. Jesus' advice to us on the subject is compelling: "Are you tired? Worn out? Burned out on religion? Come to me. Get away with me and you'll recover your life. I'll show you how to take a real rest. Walk with me and work with me—watch how I do it. Learn the unforced rhythms of grace. I won't lay anything heavy or ill-fitting on you. Keep company with me and you'll learn to live freely and lightly" (Matthew 11:28–30 THE MESSAGE).

I am a consultant psychiatrist and therefore am faced constantly with making difficult decisions at work. In the past I found it hard not to fall into doubt and self-reproach when things went wrong. I devised intricate tactics to cover this up, but in my more private moments I thought that the fault lines in my personality would eventually split me into a thousand pieces, without hope of restoration. (These times were my Humpty Dumpty moments.)

In 1997, I began attending an Alpha Course, because, uniquely for me, I had felt close to the end of life and no one seemed to understand. Only a Christian friend was able to see through my defenses and suggested I come to her Alpha group. I thought, *What the hell!* and knew I would be able to discern artificial or hysterical manifestations shown by others. I accepted the common sense wrapped up in Christian mumbo-jumbo as relatively harmless. At this time, I attended a weekend Christian conference on work-related issues. I was ready to go to the pub at the end of the proceedings, none the worse for spending two days in the company of Christians. There was an opportunity for prayer and I was happy to be able to sit with two friends who could pray harmlessly. I was quite surprised to be knocked back into my seat by a force that I identified immediately as passing through my "cartoon" heart (i.e., not at the anatomical position but closer to the center of the chest). I was filled with an irrational sense of relief, followed by joy and then intense relaxation. I now realize this was the Holy Spirit.

At work, I tried to cap any behavioral changes in case anyone asked what was wrong. However, I was impressed by the perceptiveness of many friends and colleagues who said I was so much better, so much easier to be with and to work with. Someone asked what I was "on" and where to get it. My ability to be seen as a supportive, trustworthy colleague and friend has increased. Both the clinical and academic areas of my work have benefited, with increased output of scientific papers and presentations at professional conferences. These are quantifiable results. What is even more striking, though more qualitative, is the way in which patients, relatives, and clinical colleagues respond to me. The most impressive changes have been internal. That nagging self-reproach that followed failure has all but gone.

I expected all this to wear off like any fad, but several years later my sense of God's grace, love, and immediacy is stronger than ever.

—KEN CHECINSKI, CONSULTANT PSYCHIATRIST

Recovering hope that has been impaired by failure is helped greatly when we realize that others can be helped by us. When we are going through rough times we often do not believe that we can contribute anything to helping others sort out their lives. This is not true. Often we are able to empathize far better with our colleagues who are under pressure at work when we, too, are finding life difficult. We do not need to have lives of perfect balance before we can be useful and see hope grow again. When we consciously lift our eyes above our own problems and become determined to encourage others, we find that restoration is on its way.

In summary, hope is the forgotten virtue of our age, often sandwiched between the muscularity of faith and the tenderness of love. The world needs to know that God's plan is to sum up everything in Christ, and we are the ones through whom this hope will be made known now, in our workplaces and in the world. Hope is therefore as powerful today, as it enables us to live in the present, as it will be in the future. But we have trivialized hope to the point of whimsy. Radical hope looks at the reality of hard, difficult, and sometimes impossible situations (that we encounter regularly at work) and, without ignoring these realities, empowers us in Christ to tackle them with confidence. That is the strength of the power of God at work. However, hope and perseverance go together. Without hope, why persevere? Why not live life for the moment or for immediate gain? But without perseverance, hope falls at the first time of testing.

> "HOPE IS THE FORGOTTEN VIRTUE OF OUR AGE, OFTEN SANDWICHED BETWEEN THE MUSCULARITY OF FAITH AND THE TENDERNESS OF LOVE."

We need to recover a culture of hope for our nations and our world. Starting in our workplaces, all of us can share the passion to reverse the exhaustion of hopelessness that so saps the spiritual vitality of our workplaces and our nation.

I love the story of the first performance of Oliver Messiaen's "Quartet for the End of Time." In the winter of 1941, the composer Messiaen was one of a group of French prisoners of war in Stalag VIII-A in Görlitz, Silesia. He had read the gospels and the book of Revelation and had come to believe that Jesus would return. He knew that this hope created meaning for the suffering people around him. In their appalling conditions, he understood that hope for tomorrow was essential for life today. He looked around the concentration camp and managed to gather together four instruments: a cello with a missing string, a battered violin, an old clarinet, and a piano with stuck-together keys. For this unusual combination of broken instruments, he wrote one of the greatest pieces of music of the twentieth century. Messiaen called it "Quartet for the End of Time." When it was played to five thousand prisoners of war in the freezing camp in Silesia, the audience listened with rapt attention. Messiaen wrote, "The cold was excruciating, the Stalag buried under snow, the four performers played on broken down instruments . . . But never have I had an audience who listened with such rapt attention and comprehension."[3] Those broken instruments in that unusual combination were unexpected agents of hope. Similarly, although we may feel inadequate and incomplete personally or spiritually, when we act together, God uses us to be agents of hope in the world.

MONEY AND GIVING

FOR MOST OF US, ONE OF THE RESULTS OF OUR WORK IS OUR monthly salary, and perhaps an annual bonus. Of course money is not the only reward, but somehow money is viewed differently. We react sometimes positively and sometimes guiltily to receiving it. For the most part, we try not to talk about it. What impact does the money we earn have on our life? We need money to provide for our basic material needs, but does it also bring happiness? Although most of us say that it doesn't, we feel deep down that a luxury holiday might just make all the difference. Magazines that uncover the lives of the rich and famous sell fast. Their trendsetting wardrobes, perfect children, sublime love lives, and architect-designed homes fill the pages and influence our own goals. The desire for more money has crippled many with so-called affluenza—the disease of continually wanting more. In his reflections on life, Guy de Rothschild said of money:

Everyone has it; no one has enough. Reluctant to discuss it, they think of nothing else. People invest it with their own intimate feelings, their rivalries, their triumphs, their frustrations, their ambitions, their resentments. At night it grows into something real, overpowering, enlightening, protective, crushing. A phantasmagorical god . . . it was a means, it has become an end.[1]

The prophet Haggai's description seems apt for our age: "You eat, but never have enough. You drink, but never have your fill. You put on clothes, but are not warm. You earn wages, only to put them in a purse with holes in it" (Haggai 1:6).

Financial judgments are often impaired in this pursuit of more: people find themselves burdened by absurdly large mortgages or huge monthly credit card payments. The burden of debt repayments turns money into a colossal weight, which can destroy. The 2008–09 global financial crisis brought this into sharp focus—many people were stuck with bad debt or negative equity. The purchases they thought would bring pleasure became a burden. Credit was meant to facilitate the timing of purchases. It often becomes the fuel for our greed.

EXCITEMENT AND STATUS—CAN MONEY DELIVER?

On a call-in program on the United Kingdom's Capital Radio, the presenter asked the caller, "What are you doing tonight?" He said, "Oh, I'm bored." "Why are you bored?" asked the interviewer.

"I've got no money." The caller's perception was that money would eradicate his boredom and provide excitement. Many of us put up with our week at work in anticipation of the weekend, or struggle through a year's work for the reward of a two-week holiday. Money, we believe, is a release from the grind of work.

Sir Nigel Rudd, an eminent industrialist, when asked whether money motivated him, replied, "Money buys you choices in life."[2] That is true, but which of these choices promotes happiness? At a meeting with the head of a major European communications company, I looked out of the window to see his Bentley, in which he had been driven from his yacht that had sailed from his island home. "These are not important to me," he said. "What is important is that they level the scores." Money had given him status: his possessions had become the visible public benchmark of his performance against others.

JESUS OR MONEY—WHO WILL BE MASTER?

Jesus spent over half his teaching dealing with the subject of money and possessions. This is actually far more than he taught on many other important topics such as prayer, marriage and sex, or heaven and hell. Many of his parables are about wealth, agriculture, business, debt forgiveness, and management performance—everyday examples of commerce. These teachings still form the basis for fulfilled living in a monied age. Jesus said, "No servant can serve two masters. Either he will hate the one and love the other, or he will be devoted to the one and despise the other. You cannot serve both God and Money" (Luke 16:13). Words such as "hate," "love," "despise," and "devoted" are the normal words not of commercial language but of emotion and relationship. The key question is: With whom will we have that relationship? Those who choose to serve God recognize him as master and keep money in its place. Those who don't choose God effectively choose money, and find that it masters them. Money, in this sense, is not purely nominal as economists would have it—a neutral basis for exchange—but numinous, powerful in itself. If money drives us, it tends to make us self-centered and crowds out other relationships. Our money-obsessed lives can spiral out of control. The amount of debt—both mortgages and consumer credit—that it is prudent to take on is a spiritual issue, not just an economic judgment.

Our approach to money and possessions is also a matter of geography. Jesus said, "For where your treasure is, there your heart will be also" (Matthew 6:21). We therefore need to locate precisely, using the GPS of the Spirit, where our real "treasure" lies. And treasure is simply what we value most in life. What do I really set my sights on and go after? But then we remember that Jesus tasked us in this world to build treasure in heaven. What does this mean? At its simplest, I believe we need to determine as a matter of fact what our driving

> "OUR ATTITUDE TO OUR FINANCES IS DETERMINED BY A FUNDAMENTAL CHOICE BETWEEN GOD AND MONEY, NOT BY OUR INCOME BRACKET."

motivations really are. If they are utterly selfish and materialist we need to correct them and build up acts and attitudes that are motivated by service to others. Storing up treasure in heaven (Matthew 6:20) becomes no more than the aggregation of daily acts of work well done, the proper use of money, activities undertaken in response to blessing others, and generosity when dealing with the needs of the people around us.

Our attitude to our finances is determined by a fundamental choice between God and money, not by our income bracket. Pay scales vary hugely in different fields and do not necessarily reflect the value or complexity of our work. You need only to contrast the income of a professional soccer player with that of a nurse to bring this issue into sharp focus. The point here is what we do with what we have. I once spoke to a theology student on a tight budget. I was amazed by his greed in wanting more possessions. At around the same time I was deeply touched by speaking to the leader of a missionary youth group whose personal circumstances were much the same as the student's. He and his wife showed me their budget. I could not believe the degree of their generosity, particularly as they lived by the voluntary and uncertain contributions of others.

I recall a similar conversation sitting next to a billionaire on his private jet—I was appalled by his catalogue of acquisitive desires. He was hooked on greed. And yet later, when I had advised another multibillionaire on the disposal of a major retail business for several billion dollars, I was staggered by the humility of his comments to me, the heavy responsibility he felt at being entrusted with wealth, and the total absence of greed.

In Luke 18, when Jesus met the rich young ruler, he saw that the young man's whole life was threatened because it was tied up in his "great" wealth, and thus asked him to sell everything. The man went away sad. But not everyone is called to sell everything. Indeed, in Proverbs 31, the woman is commended for setting about her work vigorously and ensuring that her trading is profitable. Jesus' story goes on with his comments on how hard it is for the rich to enter the kingdom. Commentators are divided on the precise meaning of "it is easier for a camel to go through the eye of a needle than for a rich person to enter the kingdom of God" (Luke 18:25 ESV). Like many of Jesus' sayings, it strikes me that he juxtaposed two utterly diverse images to make a similar point. It is impossible, not merely difficult, for a camel to go through the eye of a needle. (Another interpretation points to a narrow pass outside Jerusalem through which a camel could pass only if what it was carrying was taken off to enable it to squeeze through.) Either way, Jesus was clear that it would be impossible for a rich person to enter heaven. Are we therefore to conclude that heaven will be populated with the poor? Hence the middle-class angst of those around him, probably boat owners and prosperous fisherman: "Who then can be saved?" Jesus replied, "What is impossible with men is possible with God" (Luke 18:27). Following Christ in the world today is not just difficult; it is impossible. To do so we need God's help. He alone can turn the apparently impossible requirements for living righteously in a hostile world into the entirely possible way of life for Christ's followers.

Peter's reaction to Jesus' words was one of indignation: "We have left everything to follow you! What then will there be for us?" (Matthew 19:27). We can relate to his reaction. How often do we assess situations, projects, or friendships with the unexpressed, "What's in it for me?" question? The honest question of self-interest enables Jesus to give his assurance: everyone who has put him first in their relationships and in their possessions will receive a hundred times as much in this world and will inherit far more in the next (Matthew 19:29).

We should expect fair compensation for a job well done and should thus be confident yet gracious about conducting salary negotiations and asking for appropriate pay raises. Jesus made it quite clear that "the worker deserves his wages" (Luke 10:7). And Paul reinforced this message when he underlined, in three images, his passionate belief in the merits of reward for hard work. He mentioned the soldiers of the day. They were mercenaries and therefore properly entitled to be paid. He went on to ask rhetorically, "Who plants a vineyard and does not eat of its grapes? Who tends a flock and does not drink of the milk?" (1 Corinthians 9:7). He was emphatic: "When the ploughman ploughs and the thresher threshes, they ought to do so in the hope of sharing in the harvest" (v. 10). It is not possible to be effective in the workplace without a degree of personal motivation, which will involve setting targets and being rewarded for our achievements. But radical choices have to be made if our relationship with money threatens our relationship with God. Money is not evil in itself, but the lust for money is a root of all kinds of evil, trapping us in harmful desires and, ultimately, bringing about our ruin (1 Timothy 6:9–10).

GREED OR GENEROSITY—HOW DO WE DEAL WITH MONEY?

Jesus had a special concern for the marginalized and the poor. But he also ate with the rich and privileged (Luke 11:37; 14:1), enjoyed the wedding feast at Cana (John 2:1), and accepted, without demurring, the anointing with costly perfume (Matthew 26:7). He lived passionately at both ends of the human scale, not midway in a guilty compromise.

When Fi and I got married, the central theme of our marriage service was John 10:10: "I have come that they may have life, and have it to the full." We are called to the good life, but this can be enjoyed only in relationship with God and others. In this way, we need not be defensive about enjoying the financial rewards of work.

We should aim to develop Paul's ability to be contented in times of plenty and in times of need (Philippians 4:11–12). God may bless us with money, but it is not necessarily evidence of his favor. Martin Luther said, "There are three conversions necessary: the conversion of the heart, mind and the purse."[3] When Zacchaeus met Jesus, he made an immediate public declaration—straightening out his finances by giving half his money to the poor and paying back anyone he had cheated four times the amount. Jesus told him, "Today salvation has come to this house" (Luke 19:9). When we sort out our financial affairs we become open to the blessings of a full life lived as God intended. This is not a one-off event but an ongoing way of living. I am always struck by Jesus' comments on money in Luke 16:10–11. First, if you handle small amounts of money properly, then you can be trusted with large sums. But if you cut corners on small things—the VAT fiddle or cheating on the bus fare—then who will trust you in big things (v. 10)? Second, if you cannot handle money properly, who will trust you with true riches (v. 11)? The test is in small things. Small ways in which we use our money determine the trust that can be placed in us, not only by other people but also by God. I often remind myself, when I long for a deeper spiritual relationship with God, to start with the small things, for example, handling money with integrity. The material and spiritual run together in maturing a good relationship with God.

The capitalist economy relies on holding money tightly. Christ's economy is different. Hoarding resources may well inflate a bank account but will not bring with it the joy that grows out of regular giving. In some extraordinary way I have found that the more I have given, the greater have been God's blessings. That is the testimony of many Christians.

DUTY AND PRIVILEGE—WHY DO WE GIVE?

Giving belongs not to the suburbs of Christianity but to the very center of our spiritual lives. Giving is spirituality made real. Few people naturally give away their hard-earned money—it is the example of God's grace that gives us both the desire and the ability to be generous. Sometimes it is not a straight choice between keeping our money for ourselves or giving it away. Our investment decisions can take into account not just our own return but additional factors such as giving a friend a business opportunity or a place to live. One of the ways in which we get distracted from giving is when our fear of financial insecurity overwhelms a God-given desire to be generous. This is a straightforward challenge to us all. Will we live by faith or by fear? Giving is not simply a financial transaction. It is essentially an act of trust in an economic order that goes against the grain of the modern worldview. There is a struggle for supremacy between these two polarities. We clearly need to be wise and not headstrong. Not every need can be satisfied by us. We therefore need to be judicious in striking a balance between known commitments and the desire for spontaneous giving.

When the psalmist said he would honor God "above all gods" (Psalm 96:4), he was not merely stating the obvious but making it plain that there is a competitive struggle for ascendancy in our lives that goes on between the true God and the various pretenders— money, security, fufillment. The psalmist made a deliberate choice and chose the living God. We, too, need to make the same choice, even though it's not easy.

> "GIVING IS SPIRITUALITY MADE REAL."

Generous regular giving is one of the ways in which we underline to the spiritual powers that attempt to draw us away from God that we trust in him and in his control of all our resources. It is a venture of faith and therefore will be subject to attack: money can become an obstacle or a gateway to God's blessing. Giving is one of the great privileges we have and a practical way of responding to God's love. When we get our giving right, the wonderful promise of God is this: "Test me in this and see if I don't open up heaven itself to you and pour out blessings beyond your wildest dreams" (Malachi 3:10 THE MESSAGE). Here are three examples of why giving is good.

Celebration

Giving is a form of worshipping God, celebrating his goodness, and enjoying what we have. We have received blessings from him—there is no better way to respond than to be generous to others. As we thank God by being generous, it seems that our thanks can be multiplied. Paul, writing to encourage generosity in the Christians at Corinth, said, "Because of the service by which you have proved yourselves, [people] will praise God" (2 Corinthians 9:13). He also assured them, "God loves a cheerful giver" (v. 7). He wants to see the smile on our faces when we give. At HTB, where I worship, we have Gift Days when we restate our vision and ask the congregation to join in the vision by contributing financially. Bishop Sandy Millar, former vicar of HTB, who initiated this way of giving, urged us to indulge only in "hilarious giving," saying, "If you can't give with a smile, don't give at all!" Thus we make an effort to accentuate the joy of giving by having a carnival atmosphere, with accompanying music and singing as people come up to the front of the church to put their pledges into a basket. This is a deliberate liturgy that is founded in the belief that God wishes our giving to be festive rather than sullen. This joyful overflowing has spiritual significance, challenging our assumptions that giving is always covert and painful.

Freedom

Generous giving is liberating. Every time we give, we issue a defiant statement to the forces that lie behind money, saying in effect, "You don't have a hold on me." Wealth can give us the illusion of independence from God. As we grow more affluent, the temptation is to put our security in our possessions and to grow less dependent on God. By doing so, we begin to choke the life of the Spirit. Giving in the power of the Spirit is the best way that I know of breaking the potential grip of money and of keeping it in its rightful place. What we cannot give freely possesses us. Giving is the antidote to materialism.

Investment

My father was a farmer. When I watched him planting orange trees, I would say to him, "But it's going to take such a long time to get fruit." However, he was looking ahead to the harvest. He even developed a method of planting two trees next to each other in order to increase the harvest. Giving is our planting and the harvest is our righteousness (2 Corinthians 9:10). Giving is a central part of the process by which we become more like Christ—the aim of every believer. A wise pastor once asked me the disarming questions: "How Christlike are you today? How's your giving?" Being Christlike is inseparable from giving. As we give generously today we do so not only to alleviate immediate need, but also as an investment for future generations.

In Paul's teaching on giving in 2 Corinthians, he said, "Whoever sows sparingly will also reap sparingly, and whoever sows generously will also reap generously" (9:6). This echoes

Jesus' own words: "Give, and it will be given to you. . . . For with the measure you use, it will be measured to you" (Luke 6:38). Not pound sterling for pound sterling or dollar for dollar, but blessing upon blessing. God doesn't necessarily promise us financial prosperity, but he does promise to supply all our needs and he assures us of an ongoing relationship with him that lasts into eternity.

When we give, we are investing not only in our own relationship with God but also in God's wider kingdom.

My local church called an emergency meeting regarding funding. It seemed that we'd overextended ourselves in our evangelistic activities and we needed to either cut back or find a significant sum of money. As the discussion progressed, it dawned on me that we were in a very privileged position, as we were starting to see some exciting results. Other generations would have given anything for this. I realized that giving was an investment in the kingdom, not just a drain on our bank accounts. After the meeting, it was amazing to see all the money that we needed coming in from a variety of sources.

—TOM JOHNSON, CITY ANALYST

Paul is clear that the giving of the Philippian Christians is a credit to their account (Philippians 4:17–18). We have personal investment accounts that only God audits. But we should not forget that our giving is not a debit on the account but a credit. True, when we give we deduct from our bank accounts, but then immediately a credit is posted in the portfolio of investment in God's kingdom. One day the audit report will be read. It is a salutary question to ask, "Will I dread it like a bad school report, or wait eagerly for the master's, 'Well done'?"

WHO, HOW, WHEN, WHAT?—THE PRACTICALITIES OF GIVING

Giving is a work of God's grace in our lives. So we can ask God to help us to want to give. Then we just start. I regret how long it took me to establish a good life pattern of giving. Even now it's not perfect. There are always reasons, none of them good, for putting this off. Start small—start by giving money to people, causes, objectives that you feel strongly about. But just start! Giving is a habit that, once established, brings huge benefits.

Who?

It is important to think carefully and pray about the individual or organization we are proposing to give to. Once my wife and I have decided on the total amount it is right to give, we slice the cake in a fairly disciplined manner. The lion's share goes to our church. We trust the leadership to use the money wisely and feel responsible as congregation members both to help pay for boring running costs (such as heating, lighting, and administration) and to contribute to the church's vision. The next slice goes to other local or global Christian organizations that attract us personally. We are particularly keen to support evangelism before general charitable giving, as these wider initiatives have a much bigger potential pool of donors. In one sense we treat our giving like any other investment and make a point of listening to our "investment reports" (annual reports and feedback). We find it encouraging when we recognize in the lives changed the yield on our money and prayers. Paul, writing to the Philippians, thanked them for sharing in his financial troubles (Philippians 4:15). Giving cements a relationship with those who receive and gives us the opportunity to remain involved in their lives.

Although most of our giving is planned, if someone on the street asks me for money, I usually give, largely as a ministry to myself. Some people object that these individuals will just get their next fix. Perhaps. Perhaps not. But to give in this way is a constant reminder of how difficult it is to part with money and how generous God is. However small the amount we give, it builds a sustainable pattern of generosity.

How?

The Pharisees wanted others to see their giving; they were rebuked for their ostentation. Some giving should be anonymous— the left hand not knowing what the right hand is doing (Matthew 6:3). On other occasions, it is right to make clear the source of the gift. This is not to invite a debtor relationship. Rather, it is to demonstrate the body of Christ working to meet each other's needs. Christ is honored when the known needs of Christians are met by other Christians. One of the highlights of our church year is a week away all together every summer (called Focus). Each year we give out scholarships to people who otherwise couldn't afford to come and we have a collection on the final day to cover the costs. Those who have more give so that those who have less are able to come. One mother whose whole family came on a scholarship said afterward, "I just can't explain how amazing it was that we could go!" Everything changed for that family a few months later, though, when they inherited some money. One of the first things they did was give some of it to the church, so that other people could be helped as they had been. The mother said, "I praise God for his generosity to us, which has enabled us to give. It is our honor and joy to give to HTB."

But it is not always money that needs to be given, as Bees Harris comments:

> As a nurse, I accept that my shift patterns sometimes involve working over the weekend. However, wherever possible, I request Sundays off so that I can help with the church youth group. I've decided that this is a priority—so it's worth forfeiting the enhanced Sunday rate.
>
> —BEES HARRIS, STAFF NURSE

We can also give our skills, time, and energy, or share our possessions. If we have a spare room in our home that could provide accommodation, we can offer it. If we have a garden, we can let others enjoy it. If we have a car, we can insure someone else to drive it. At all times, we need to be wise about sharing, setting limits to avoid abuse and to protect our families.

When?

There is undoubtedly a blessing that comes from regular giving. "On the first day of every week, each one of you should set aside a sum of money in keeping with your income" (1 Corinthians 16:2). Whenever our money comes in, we should set aside a sum proportionate to what we are earning. This should be the first, rather than the last, deduction. Like many other payments, such as mortgages or credit cards, giving regularly is best. Impulse giving is good but not sufficient. We need to plan the bulk of our giving while leaving room for moments of spontaneous generosity.

What?

In the New Testament we are not told the precise amount that we should give. At one level, this is strange. Both Jesus and Paul had ample opportunity to reinforce the tithe message. Paul could of course have assumed it in his teaching on financial giving, but perhaps "the apostle of the free spirit" was making a wider and more momentous point by his silence: generosity is not quantifiable. Instead, most of the teaching focuses on our attitude. It is inconceivable to Jesus that we should have a loving heart and not show this by our actions. "You give a tenth of your spices. . . . But you have neglected the more important matters of the law—justice, mercy and faithfulness. You should have practiced the latter, without neglecting the former" (Matthew 23:23). There is a hint here that a tithe (the 10 percent) is taken for granted, but equally this is a passage not on tithing, but on attitudes and transparency.

I am often asked about tithing. Behind the question is partly a desire for a biblical view, but also the longing for certainty. I believe that, although the prescriptive rules on tithing were appropriate for a non-welfare state economy in Old and New Testament times, they remain a good practical guide for giving today. Of course, if our salaries increase, we should revise our giving upward, always aiming to be generous and not duty-bound.

Giving inevitably brings about a drop in our standard of living. Anybody who gives generously will have less for other material things but will find their lives greatly enriched.

At times, particularly during economic uncertainty and crisis, people get into a mess financially and find themselves in debt. (By debt, I am not referring to long-term prudent mortgage repayments, which are a normal part of people's lives.) So what do we do about giving if we are in financial crisis? I believe that getting out of debt as quickly as possible is the best way to honor God. I would advise talking to someone trustworthy in order, first, to acknowledge the problem and, second, to establish a credible plan to resolve it. In the short term, everything other than true essentials should be suspended. I would suspend giving only temporarily—as part of a program of quite drastic lifestyle cutbacks—and would never stop giving without knowing when I planned to start again. It can also be helpful to mark the fact that we are back on track financially and free to be generous with our money again with a one-off celebratory donation.

I think it is important to talk about money, but we need to do so carefully and sensitively, choosing the right people with whom to share our financial information. When I was trying to establish a healthy pattern of giving, I talked regularly with one friend who I felt understood my situation. I trusted him and found his calm and steady manner particularly reassuring.

What then, in summary, should be our attitude to money? Is it filthy lucre that will contaminate us, or is it a force for good? Of its own it is neither: it is our attitude to its use that will govern which it is to be. That is why thankful, regular, and cheerful giving is so important. Not only does it honor God's name, but expectant giving also enables us to rely on God's promise to "meet all your needs according to his glorious riches in Christ Jesus" (Philippians 4:19). The net result is that we experience the freedom to enjoy our possessions, our money, our holidays, our gadgets, and our cars. Giving frees us up to enjoy God's goodness precisely because our priorities are right as we provide first for the needs of others and then for ourselves.

God, "who richly provides us with everything for our enjoyment," also tells us to be "willing to share" (1 Timothy 6:17–18). There is therefore every good reason for us to enjoy material benefits in proportion to the way we live, the generosity of our giving, and our gratitude to God, the provider. This attitude leads to the responsible enjoyment of our possessions. A good indication that we have the balance right is that we are able to enjoy both what we have and what we give.

There is, as ever, much practical wisdom in Proverbs on the subject of money and possessions. Proverbs 23:4 is a reminder to all of us: "Do not wear yourself out to get rich; have the wisdom to show restraint. Cast but a glance at riches, and they are gone, for they will surely sprout wings and fly off to the sky like an eagle."

In conclusion, it is worth looking at an extract from John Wesley's brilliant sermon "The Use of Money."

Gain all you can, without hurting either yourself or your neighbor, in soul or body, by applying hereto with unintermitted diligence, and with all the understanding which God has given, you; save all you can by cutting off every expense which serves only to indulge foolish desire, to gratify either the desire of the flesh, the desire of the eye, or the pride of life; waste nothing, living or dying, on sin or folly, whether for yourself or your children; and then, give all you can, or, in other words, give all you have to God. Do not stint yourself . . . to this or that proportion. "Render unto God," not a tenth, not a third, not half, but all that is God's, be it more or less; by employing all on yourself, your household, the household of faith, and all mankind, in such a manner, that you may give a good account of your stewardship when ye can be no longer stewards.[4]

SPIRITUAL RENEWAL

VICENTE FOX, WHILE PRESIDENT OF MEXICO, ADDRESSED A GATHER-ing of business and political leaders at the World Economic Forum with these words:

> No aspect of contemporary life is more notable and less understood than the spiritual discontent and restlessness that is spreading worldwide. This unease is present among those who are safe and wealthy as well as among the poor and desperate. We can now see throughout the world a rejection of crass materialism and an intense undirected desire for spiritual rebirth.[1]

Finding meaning and purpose in life is, I believe, the greatest challenge of our time. This search is as essential to establishing lasting peace, sustainable economic activity, and strong communities at ease with each other as any of the other major challenges of climate change, elimination of extreme poverty, or globalization.

Fox described the desire for renewal as "intense." I believe he is right. There is a new intensity in the search for values and a meaningful way of life. The surge in spiritual hunger, particularly among young people, has increased and the institutional church has largely found itself unable to provide the necessary food. So many people's searches continue without guidance— "undirected." Within the church, the "official guides" are taken up in a distracting internal agenda of their own relating to the role of women, sexuality, and other parochial agendas— debates that seem irrelevant to most. For many, therefore, this undirected search leads merely into the dead ends of contemporary fads.

At the end of 2005, Her Majesty the Queen addressed the General Synod of the Church of England and reminded us of this hunger for meaning in today's society:

> When so much is in flux, when limitless amounts of information, much of it ephemeral, are instantly accessible on demand, there is a renewed hunger for that which endures and gives meaning. The Christian church can speak uniquely to that need for, at the heart of our faith, stands the conviction that all people, irrespective of race, background or circumstances, can find lasting significance and purpose in the gospel of Jesus Christ. Forgiveness lies at the heart of the Christian faith. It can heal broken families. It can restore

friendships and it can reconcile divided communities. It is in forgiveness that we feel the power of God's love.[2]

I have written this book from a Christian point of view at a time when there is a global resurgence of faith not confined to Christianity. Every boardroom, workplace, and community will therefore have to grapple with the challenges of respect for different faiths and interfaith dialogue if they are to respond positively to this worldwide phenomenon. Faith, far from being a delusion capable of being dismissed as irrelevant to the modern workplace, will increasingly become a value to be nurtured as enlightened corporations rightly accentuate the importance of diversity at work.

The truth is that God is at work in his world. He is shaking and shaping its future. We remember the words of the Lord's Prayer, which remind us that his will is done on earth as it is in heaven. "Earth" comes first—I believe deliberately, as a reminder of our priorities to be rooted in this world. He has chosen us to show that "spirituality" starts with God and has a clear mission: to bring healing and restoration to a fragmented society. He does so by holding together all our activities. I am repeatedly struck by the understanding that the Lord of compassion is also the Lord of commerce; the Lord of prayer is also the Lord of profit; and the Lord of mission is also the Lord of the money markets. He takes charge of the whole of creation and of all our endeavors. Finding spiritual renewal in a relationship with him is the key to fulfilled living but comes only when we recognize that wisdom starts with God. Wisdom is his unique spirituality for the world.

How do we recognize God at work in us? Irenaeus, the early church leader, said, "The glory of God is a human being fully alive."[3] Are we fully alive to God, willing to be molded by the Holy Spirit?

The actor Michael Caine was once asked to differentiate between a movie star and a great movie actor. His reply was instructive: "The movie star says, 'How can I change the script and story line to fit my personality?' The great actor says, 'How can I change my personality to fit the script and to do justice to the story?'"[4] If we want to be written into God's script for the world, we need to be prepared to change. We need to be willing to yield our programs to his priorities. We need a spirituality that is neither rigid nor static, nor compartmentalized, but which grows and deepens into every aspect of our lives, bringing profound inner peace. Such connectedness distinguishes Christian spirituality from other efforts at calm and peace. God is always at work, changing us, if we let him do so. He is committed to work in us, only through us. He is not the control freak chief executive. In the film *Junebug*, the wife turns to her husband and says, "God loves you just the way you are, but he loves you too much to let you stay that way." [5] As a contemporary summary of theology this sentence is unbeatable. Many questions are raised by faith and spirituality in the modern world. But there is evidence that faith is growing. The global financial crisis forced many to think beyond wealth creation and the purely economic to provide meaning and purpose. This augurs well for the future. I recently had lunch with a chairman of a large listed company. At the end of lunch, he turned to me and said that he had been reviewing his life. There were several boxes. The first was work and he felt—rightly in my view—that he had been a success. The second was his family relationships. He had been divorced and had made a special effort to ensure that his relationships with the children of his first marriage and his new family were good. This had not been easy but he felt that this was a part of his life under control. Another box he marked "friendships." During the last year he had paid particular attention to his friends, especially those who in the ceaseless demands of the workplace might have been neglected. He felt enriched by these efforts to rekindle these friendships from university and elsewhere. Then he turned to me and said, "But there is one box that is unfilled.

I don't know what to call it. But it would have something to do with the spiritual. I need to make sense of this non-material aspect of my life as I suspect it will give a key to a fuller meaning to the other parts of my life. Somehow this is the missing part of my life."

Connectivity is one of the great drivers of modern technology. This is demonstrated by the speed with which computers can talk to each other and data can be carried. Similarly, the Holy Spirit is the connector, the fluid and frictionless link between humanity and its Creator.

We all know the frustration of losing the connection when we are online and the delight of mobile broadband keeping us linked in. In earlier translations of John's gospel, Jesus calls us to "Abide in me" (John 15:4 ESV). "Staying connected" might be the modern translation. A true connectedness to God is the secret of successful living in the workplace and will transform our relationships at work. The starting point is not our religion but our common humanity—precisely the point of God's connection with us through the incarnation. If we demonstrate that we are completely and sacrificially "for" our colleagues, perhaps Christians will cease to be known for what they are against.

As Christians, we are, in a wider sense, for society and not against it. We are called to be part of a wider social and moral order that is worth fighting for and defending. The prevailing structure is based on an atomized view of life, which celebrates an individualistic ethic, demonstrated by the widespread pursuit of possessions. But to seek riches without caring for others is ultimately to experience poverty. We are impoverished whenever the wider interests of humanity are excluded from our day-to-day working lives. We cannot live in a world of extreme poverty and not wish to act to redress this injustice.

There is a haunting judgment in Malachi 2:2 in which God says to the people of Israel that if they disregard his ways "[he] will curse [their] blessings." We see each day the tragic consequences of the way we have inflicted this judgment upon ourselves. Western lifestyles are largely prosperous, yet our family life is fragmenting before our very eyes. We have a chronic fear of the future. We are frightened in our streets as crimes against the person grow, and in a myriad of ways we see the tapestry of our society torn beyond recognition by the unrestrained forces of consumerism, greed, and envy. How do we weave back into the tapestry the broken threads that once again could illustrate a true picture of God reflected in our places of work and the society around us?

The answer to these questions lies in a new discovery of radical hardcore Christianity—a faith that has been stripped to its essentials. The Holy Spirit who reminds the world of its need for God (John 16:8) is not only the instrument of judgment but also the binding agent who links our lives at work to a greater social movement that we call the kingdom of God, and which we long to see taking root on earth.

This movement underpins the communities in which we work, regards the stability that comes from family life as the first building block for a sustained society, accepts accountability in public affairs as essential for the economy to flourish, and yet hears the cries of the marginalized, the poor and disadvantaged, and takes seriously all efforts to eradicate the extremes of global poverty. This is a movement that is not based on muddle-headed economics but has the true ingredients of a productive and compassionate social order that most closely reflects the true freedom of the New Testament.

This is a movement that could close society's "gaps." For example, in the UK a significant majority of people believe in God, but few of these enjoy the benefits of being active followers. How can we narrow this gap when we have failed to provide an attractive model for living authentic Christian lives? How can we eradicate the distinction between sacred and secular that has created such a harmful passivity among Christians? How can we narrow the gap between extreme poverty and rich nations, between domestic protection and global free trade, and between those who hope in God and those who live without hope?

Bridging these gaps is a Trinitarian imperative. God

embraced those who were anti-God because he wished to close the gap that had arisen between the vitality of the Godhead, reflected in the first Creation, and the miserable lives lived by those who turned from him. God was interested in community well before he became interested in the church.

> "NOTHING SHORT OF A NEW PENTECOST—AN OUTPOURING OF THE SPIRIT THAT BRINGS NEWNESS, CREATIVITY, AND ADVENTURE—IS REQUIRED IF WE ARE TO SEE OUR PLACES OF WORK TRANSFORMED, OUR COMMUNITIES THROBBING WITH LIFE, AND OUR SOCIETY HEALED."

The task is so immense that nothing short of a new Pentecost—an outpouring of the Spirit that brings newness, creativity, and adventure—is required if we are to see our places of work transformed, our communities throbbing with life, and our society healed. Herein lies true prosperity. We cannot achieve much on our own and will become dispirited, but with the Holy Spirit there is enormous power.

I thank God for the privilege of living as a witness for him at the start of the twenty-first century. I would wish to live at no other time in history—not even in Judea at the time of Jesus. Opportunities for spreading the good news have never been greater. The real economic cost of travel and communication is declining year by year. The message does not have to be contained geographically or through lack of communication. Modern technology makes it possible to spread the good news more effectively than ever before. The challenge will be to ensure that we can use the advantages of technology, instant communication, and social media to execute a coherent strategy for returning the workplace to its roots of faith-based values. Close observation of chief executives of global corporations shows that they fail not because of a lack of vision, but for a lack of delivering results. Getting things done is one of the great requirements of success in modern business. This is also true of the church, and ordinary Christians need to get on with the job of transforming the workplace and the nation. This is central to our mission to the world. The task of recovering a whole-of-life faith is not one that can be delegated to bishops and church leaders. At a time of crisis in the church, a fresh lay initiative is needed to reconnect the workplace with Christianity. There are enormous spiritual and economic benefits to be gained from restoring purpose and value to our workplaces. We can easily work in not-for-profit organizations: we cannot, however, work in not-for-purpose organizations. If we are not convinced of the purpose of our work, we will never work well and enjoy it.

The last book that Pope John Paul II wrote before he died was a reflection of Jesus'

> "THERE ARE ENORMOUS SPIRITUAL AND ECONOMIC BENEFITS TO BE GAINED FROM RESTORING PURPOSE AND VALUE TO OUR WORKPLACES."

call of John 14:31: "Get up. Let's go. It's time to leave here" (THE MESSAGE). We are all on a journey and will not be able to locate every point on the map. We are utterly reliant on the Holy Spirit to show us the way. We do not have to fear the world, because of Jesus' promise: "Take heart! I have overcome the world" (John 16:33). The task is enormous but the promise of fulfilled living and the restoration of the values with which God started our world is a huge prize. We will never make any progress without recognizing that we are sustained by his grace. If we are to see our society truly transformed and our nation turned to God, it will come about only when the people at work rise to this vision. We are the unseen army of connectors touching millions of people each day. As we re-engage with people at work, we could see a viral explosion of faith. The missionary effect of Christians at work living authentic lives, weak yet empowered by the Holy Spirit, vulnerable yet strengthened by God, anxious yet filled with peace, could, through a new outpouring of God's Spirit, become the greatest evangelistic movement of our age.

AFTERMATH: THE MORAL SPIRIT IN LIGHT OF THE FINANCIAL CRISIS

WHEN LEHMAN BROTHERS FILED FOR BANKRUPTCY ON SEPTEMBER 15, 2008, everyone knew that this was an unprecedented event. The investment bank was more than 150 years old and was the fourth largest in the United States. Bankruptcy should not ever have cast a shadow over such a prestigious, successful firm. The unthinkable had happened.

The US government's decision not to bail out the bank signaled a change of weather in the financial world. As Lehman Brothers was going under, Merrill Lynch had to be rescued with a buyout by Bank of America. A few days later, the insurance giant AIG was saved with an $85 billion bailout. The following month, Royal Bank of Scotland (RBS) and Lloyds approached the UK government seeking a bailout worth £37 billion. This was clearly no financial tremor but a major earthquake, bringing down some of the most secure institutions in the financial world. The aftershocks of these crises are still being felt as the banking crisis continues. In fact, the debt crisis left no one untouched. Household debt, banking debt, and sovereign debt showed that every level of society was tainted.

Since the 2008–09 financial crash, many books have been published outlining different explanations for the catastrophe. Yet all of them agree on at least one premise: one of the largest problems was the sheer complexity of financial products and the trading system.

For too long, bankers had mistaken complexity for progress. They somehow came to believe that the more complicated a financial process was, the better and more reliable it must be. Incomprehensible algorithms became a symbol of confidence and security, yet in fact it was this complexity in which this system's vulnerability lay. "Did no one see this coming?" asked the queen at a meeting at the London School of Economics regarding the financial crisis.[1] The question remains unanswered.

This in itself was symbolic of a much longer-standing trend in economic thinking. For many years, economics had tried to turn itself into a hard, objective science, totally grounded in mathematical equations and, significantly, free from subjective and personal judgment. This apparently gave economists a sense of confidence, reliability, and respectability. Economics became totally separate from values, morality, character, relationships, or anything concrete, everyday, and ordinary. It was about science, mathematics, calculations, and equations. The prevailing mind-set of the time was that economics was much the better for it.

The only problem with this outlook is that it was nonsense. The search for a system that was perfectly rational, objective, and logical was the financial equivalent of the search for the Holy Grail. And it stood about as much chance of success. We have tried to dream up a financial system that is so perfect that no one needs to be good.

> "WE HAVE TRIED TO DREAM UP A FINANCIAL SYSTEM THAT IS SO PERFECT THAT NO ONE NEEDS TO BE GOOD."

"Purely objective policy is not possible," remarked two MPs with extensive experience in the money markets. Or, put another way, you cannot take the human out of the economic. Those same MPs observed that, with financial equations, as with so much else in life, if you put "garbage in, [you get] garbage out."

There is, of course, nothing wrong with rigor and objectivity, or even with complex mathematical calculations and equations. But to imagine that you can cut the human—to cut the ethical— out of the system is to make a profound error. Back in the 1930s T. S. Eliot wrote in his play *Choruses from the Rock* about how people "constantly try to escape" from the "unpleasant facts" of life, "by dreaming of systems so perfect that no one will need to be good."[2] At the time, he was referring to those communist systems that tried to build heaven on earth and ended up with hell. But the lesson remains for us today. We need to reconnect the financial world with its ethical foundation in a way that requires more than simply greater regulation and legislation, for humans are *moral* beings as much as they are *financial* ones. Michael Sandel, professor of philosophy at Harvard University, delivered the prestigious BBC Reith Lectures in 2009. He said, "Markets have become so detached from fundamental values, that we need to reconnect markets and values."[3] And British prime minister David Cameron commented in a speech to the World Economic Forum, "It is time to place the market within a moral framework."[4]

WHAT THE WORLD NEEDS

Regulation on its own will not make a good financial system, at least not if you understand the word *good* to have some moral significance, rather than simply being another word for "efficient." But we cannot hope to run a secure, efficient, or sustainable finance sector if we fail to realize that we also need *unwritten* laws of conduct—basic human values—just as much as we need written ones, in the form of regulation and legislation. The bottom line is that we need more than the bottom line.

We need business leaders who can combine profitability and the long view that makes profitability sustainable, and to do that we need new forms of leadership. I suggest that we should think of the leader as steward, the person who can carry the community with him or her but who earns legitimacy from managing resources for the long-term benefit of all. If financial and other leaders had acted as stewards of the long term, the crash caused by excessive short-term speculation would never have blighted so many lives. It is therefore *visionary* leadership that we need, for it is able to see further, more clearly, earlier, and differently—without losing sight of the moral responsibility to make a profit and create jobs.

In addition, bankers—just like politicians, and indeed everyone else involved in any way in the crisis—need to respond *morally*: by adopting a new basis, a new perspective for finance—one that is deeply and explicitly ethical. Therefore, the softer, subtler, cultural values of honor, honesty, integrity, and decency are essential—at least as essential as effective legislation. Or put

> "WE CANNOT HOPE TO RUN A SECURE, EFFICIENT, OR SUSTAINABLE FINANCE SECTOR IF WE FAIL TO REALIZE THAT WE NEED UNWRITTEN LAWS OF CONDUCT."

another way, we need the law—but not as much as we need the spirit of the law. Soon after the financial crisis hit, I was asked to give a number of talks from a Christian perspective on the implications of the financial crisis. The lessons that were to be learned in the heat of the crisis are the same ones we need to learn now.

I was particularly struck by the message contained in the letter to the Hebrews:

"One last shaking, from top to bottom, stem to stern." The phrase "one last shaking" means a thorough house cleaning, getting rid of all the historical and religious junk so that the

unshakable essentials stand clear and uncluttered. . . . God
is . . . actively cleaning house, torching all that needs to burn,
and he won't quit until it's all cleansed. (Hebrews 12:26–29
THE MESSAGE)

The search is for that which is unshakable. Very few pillars
of our economic life have not been subject to severe testing. That
is the good news. The financial crisis has forced us to determine
what is of lasting importance and what is not. Unfortunately,
when such a massive shaking occurs, those who have built their
houses upon the sand of false hopes will naturally find the slip-
page almost unbearable.

Is there any warning in the Bible of what happens when a
financial system gets out of kilter in this way? An answer lies in
Ezekiel 27 with a description of the Mediterranean city of Tyre.
The city was the "gateway to the sea, merchant to the world" (v.
3 THE MESSAGE). It was at the hub of financial and commercial
transactions in the region. Ezekiel described people "clustered
around you to barter for your goods" (v. 9 THE MESSAGE). The
impression is given of enormous wealth, great skill, huge reputation, and immense pride. Yet financial success did not last:
"Your worldwide trade made earth's kings rich. And now you're
battered to bits by the waves, sunk to the bottom of the sea. . . .
The buyers and sellers of the world throw up their hands: This
horror can't happen! Oh, this *has* happened!" (Ezekiel 27:33–36
THE MESSAGE, emphasis added).

Tyre could so easily have been the city of London, or Wall
Street, or Tokyo. The description of the highways of the seas,

captured so picturesquely by Ezekiel, could find modern expression in the digital communications that lead to the trillions of dollars that are traded each day and the products that criss-cross today's financial world.

In the following chapter, in response to Tyre's extraordinary pride, Ezekiel brings a message from God to give a reason for the absolute collapse of the city, which, having ridden high, was brought completely low. These reasons are as trenchant to Tyre as they are to us.

First, "Your heart is proud, going around saying, 'I'm a god'" (Ezekiel 28:2 THE MESSAGE). It is not fanciful to imagine that finance and economics had been elevated to such a high degree as to deify them, thinking they were capable of answering all our issues. How these verses resonate: "Your sharp intelligence made you world-wealthy. You piled up gold and silver in your banks. You used your head well, worked good deals, made a lot of money, but the money has gone to your head, swelled your head—what a big head!" (vv. 4–5 THE MESSAGE). And then the Lord answered, "Because you're acting like a god, pretending to be a god, I'm giving fair warning. . . . [I'll] puncture the balloon of your god-pretensions" (vv. 6–7 THE MESSAGE).

This passage shows what happens when individuals or societies try to run their affairs without reference to God. Ultimately, if there is no restraint, arrogance will cause a shaking or a stumbling. As it was in Tyre, so it will be with us today. It is therefore imperative for us to reconnect the values that are important for us as a society to the underlying commercial performances.

I once commented to a fellow banker that during the crisis,

bankers were becoming like gods—as Ezekiel warned. Banks, unlike other manufacturers, have one extraordinary common feature with divinity, which is why the parallel is so apt. They can create credit *ex nihilo*, in much the same way as God created the world from nothing. That is what banks do. Credit is made by a decision of the board of directors of a bank, subject to the regulatory and shareholder demands in force at the time. Bankers were prepared to see the creation of the vast amount of credit that so swamped the world and brought down its financial systems. And like Tyre, they were not prepared to assume the responsibility that came with this quasi-creator role. Unlike the true God, they were prepared to create this economic bubble of apparent strength over the last decade, but were unable, or unwilling, to shoulder the accompanying responsibilities. When the true God created the world, he not only did so, but also assumed responsibility for the whole of creation. In this respect, the crashing of the financial system, like that of Tyre, was the ultimate hubris of human creators, unable to control that which they had brought into being.

RECONNECTING THE FINANCIAL WITH THE HUMAN

We should make no mistake: there is a cloud of public frustration with the failure to connect finance and values, under which we are all sitting. If we ignore it, it shows every sign of growing and darkening. There is also the idea that the only social responsibility of business is to increase its profits. This idea has been highly influential for many years and it is, I believe, profoundly misguided.

Businesses employ human beings. Their products and services inform and shape human society. Their operations are embedded within human communities.

The idea that business is about profit *rather than* people, and that the rules of the game are *legal* rather than *moral*, is to put the financial and ethical parts of human beings into separate silos. It is to imagine that we are profit-seekers on weekdays and parents, friends, neighbors, and citizens on weekends.

If the global financial crisis has taught us anything, it is that you simply cannot split the financial from the human. Ultimately, if we fragment human beings, we will end up with a fragmented, perhaps even a broken, society.

THE SPIRIT OF THE LAW

When the crisis is expressed in this way, the connection between Christianity and the financial and business world becomes clearer.

Jesus, throughout his ministry, leveled his energies against the law, not in itself, but the spirit in which it was interpreted and implemented. Although it should have been a vehicle for love, generosity, thankfulness, and life, it had become a vehicle of oppression and judgment.

> "TO MAKE OUR WORKPLACES GOOD WE NEED THE RIGHT SPIRIT—THE RIGHT ETHICAL SPIRIT."

Economies need legislation. Banks need regulation. And businesses need good codes of conduct.

However, all of them also need the right spirit. Neither legislation nor regulation nor codes of conduct will make us, or our workplaces, *good*. For that we need the right spirit—the *right ethical spirit*.

SEEING THINGS DIFFERENTLY

If this seems unrealistic or naïve—the idea that, if we shine like ethical stars in the workplace, all shall be well—it's worth being clear about what this does and does not mean. It's also worth reminding ourselves that the world is a messy place filled with harsh commercial compromise, ambiguity, and daily dilemmas.

First, it doesn't mean we should "preach," or moralize, or continually pass judgment on one another's working lives. It is one of the tragedies of our time that we instantly associate morality with moralizing. What it does mean is seeing things differently. What I mean by this is perhaps best illustrated by a story from Numbers 13 that has already been considered earlier in the book.

The Lord said to Moses, "Send some men to explore the land of Canaan, which I am giving to the Israelites" (v. 1). He explicitly instructed that they should come "from each ancestral tribe [who should] send one of its leaders" (v. 2). It is a broad, nationally inclusive, specific mission.

Moses duly obeyed and sent twelve people from each of the tribes, including Caleb and Joshua. He told them to go through the Negev or desert region and up into the hill country. This is a reconnaissance party. In Numbers 13:18–20 Moses instructed them,

See what the land is like and whether the people who live there are strong or weak, few or many. What kind of land do they live in? Is it good or bad? What kind of towns do they live in? Are they unwalled or fortified? How is the soil? Is it fertile or poor? Are there trees on it or not? Do your best to bring back some of the fruit of the land.

Moses was clear what he wanted people to *see*—and as if we haven't gotten the message, the author then went into forensic detail about where the explorers go, listing the places in turn.

Why did the author give so much detail? I suggest it is to convey that all the explorers saw the same very real and concrete things, even down to the smallest details describing the pomegranates and figs.

This is important because of what happened next. The explorers came back to Moses and Aaron and the whole Israelite community and reported to them. But this is when the crunch comes. The spies had all seen the same things but they had not seen them in the same way. In a dramatic turning point in the story, the author tells us that "Caleb silenced the people before Moses" and then said, "We should go up and take possession of the land, for we can certainly do it" (v. 30).

However, this is not what the others were thinking. They said, "We can't attack those people; they are stronger than we are." Doubt spread through the Israelites' camp. "The land we explored devours those living in it," they said. "All the people we saw there are of great size" (vv. 31–32). The majority report destroyed morale and the people effectively rebelled against Moses and Aaron. "We should choose a leader and go back to Egypt," they said (Numbers 14:4). At this point Caleb (and Joshua) spoke up.

> Joshua . . . and Caleb . . . , *who were among those who had explored the land . . .* said to the entire Israelite assembly, "The land we passed through and explored is exceedingly good. If the LORD is pleased with us, he will lead us into that land." (vv. 6–8 emphasis added)

In one respect this is simply courage. But it is important to recognize that courage doesn't exist like some free-floating value. It has—indeed it needs—secure foundations to support it. We need a reason to be courageous.

The foundation of Joshua and Caleb's courage is their trust in God. They have seen the same as the other spies—after all, they "were among those who had explored the land"—but they had seen it with different eyes, with the eyes informed by faith.

Unless we understand human nature and behavior *as it really is*—and not as we like to imagine it to be—we are liable to repeat the severe financial crash of recent years again and again. Humans being what we are, governments cannot simply let the market rule. Working free markets require strong frameworks of values to underpin their effectiveness, and markets alone do not generate such a framework.

Humans are indeed capable of much, but we are all, nonetheless, stubbornly human. The Bible is clear that we all are of one stock—a key insight, by the way, that inspired William Wilberforce and his campaign to abolish slavery. We are all imbued with an inherent dignity, capacity to choose, the desire for freedom, and the need to love and be loved. It is to claim that, however much we try to wriggle out of it, we exist in a moral dimension, condemned to knowing good and evil and being ethically responsible for our actions. We have what I have called a financial spirit—the desire to do well—but we also have a moral spirit—the desire to do good. And if we are able to recognize this ineradicable moral element of human nature, then bringing God to work will seem less daunting. If you have eyes to see, you will notice that there are signs of God, and of the good, in places where you might not otherwise expect to find them.

RELEARNING THE LANGUAGE OF VALUES

What does this mean in practice? Well, we have lost the grammar of ethical discourse and need to relearn the language of values. The crisis of trust brought into existence since the global financial crisis is an opportunity to build an economy that realigns the ethical with the financial, the public interest with private gain. As described earlier in the book, my work with London Connection seeks to realign these seemingly

> "IF YOU HAVE EYES TO SEE, YOU WILL NOTICE THAT THERE ARE SIGNS OF GOD, AND OF THE GOOD, IN PLACES WHERE YOU MIGHT NOT OTHERWISE EXPECT TO FIND THEM."

contradictory aspects. The market economy must not ignore the voices of those for whom it is not working. We need to reconnect our communities.

For a whole host of reasons—some flimsy, some sound—we have grown shy of doing morality in public. Nobody likes being accused of moralizing or being judgmental (perhaps the gravest modern-day sin), and nobody likes being accused of hypocrisy (which is a great deal more likely if you become associated with a particular moral code).

> "WE NEED TO RELEARN THE LANGUAGE OF VALUES."

However, we *are* moral creatures and we cannot live, let alone flourish, unless we recognize that publicly. We need to become more comfortable thinking and talking about moral values in public. Some things are right, some are wrong; some behavior is acceptable, some unacceptable; some actions are good, some are not; some cultures are generous and forgiving, others are hard and merciless. Pretending things aren't so, simply because we are shy of using moral value language in public, does nobody any good. It merely hides the obvious, failing to give the good its proper due, or to give the bad its proper warning. Businesses cannot work, banks cannot lend, economies cannot function, and societies cannot flourish without mutual trust, honesty, and integrity.

If we do start talking values, I suspect we will find that the values we talk will chime with what most people instinctively feel about how to live well in life: be honest; live with integrity; place trust; generate wealth; look to do well; treat employees and colleagues as humans, not as units of production; treat suppliers fairly; operate as a responsible neighbor in the community; recognize your wider social obligations; protect the environment for future generations, and so on. We have much to gain and much less to lose by bringing the moral spirit into the workplace.

Talking, however, is not enough. Indeed, talking values without living them is part of the problem and has its own specific name: hypocrisy.

In 1999, two consultants carrying out a yearlong project to produce a business strategy for HM Customs and Excise asked a question: Do organizational values actually matter to staff? The results of the survey were telling. The more staff felt that the organization's values fit their own, the higher their level of job satisfaction. Conversely, those with a low sense of fit were less satisfied. People "want[ed] to feel that the organization they work for is in tune with their values."[5]

> "BUSINESSES CANNOT WORK, BANKS CANNOT LEND, ECONOMIES CANNOT FUNCTION, AND SOCIETIES CANNOT FLOURISH WITHOUT MUTUAL TRUST, HONESTY, AND INTEGRITY."

In addition to this, it is worth considering that research consistently shows that, when it comes to organizational performance, a serious commitment to values does actually work. Having strong values also helps to mitigate the dangers of risk. In an international survey covering 365 companies, 90 percent of senior executives argued that a strong corporate statement of values was critical in encouraging individual employees to take action and inform their managers when something seemed wrong.[6] It was this kind of environment that prevented errors from turning into disasters. Values should chime with what most people instinctively feel: seek to be profitable; treat employees fairly; treat them equitably; treat them with respect; operate as a responsible neighbor in the community; and protect the environment for future generations.

Christians have a great opportunity to show the love of Christ, even in the midst of major financially seismic disruption. When our values are secure and we have a hope that is unshakable in Christ, we are then able to weather the shaking and reorder our own lives, determining the priorities that are important to hold to, and those values without which our lives would lose their meaning.

A young executive asked me how to respond to the financial crisis in a personal way. The answer I gave him was one that I apply to myself: determine what it is that you cannot live without, or without which your life would lack meaning, and then determine what you *can* live without. This exercise can be an important corrective. Too often in the hurly-burly since the new millennium, people have focused on financial reward to the exclusion of family relationships, friendships, and involvement in their community. When the financial edifice collapsed, these apparently softer supports came under threat. They need to be reviewed and strengthened, as they are of lasting importance.

CONCLUSION

How we behave every day with colleagues, clients, suppliers, shareholders, regulators, and customers is crucially important. While we may feel that the environment in which we work is devoid of values, if we can see with the right eyes, we will notice that every workplace is made of people and all people are made up, to a greater or lesser extent, of a moral spirit.

More to the point, today's workplace—in the wake of the biggest financial crash and some of the biggest moral failings in many decades—is uniquely open to the discovery of a moral spirit. Despite human beings' best attempts to prove to the contrary, there really is no point trying to regulate or legislate goodness into existence. If we did, the rule book would make the current book of City Regulation look like a tweet.

There is an old business consultants' saying, "Culture eats strategy for breakfast." In other words, no matter how much effort you pour into your corporate strategy, if your corporate culture is not working in line with it, you might as well be pouring money down the drain. We can adopt and adapt the same saying for this chapter: "Morality—or, perhaps more accurately, immorality—eats regulation for breakfast." Morality is our medium, the water in which we swim. More so for Christians, as we have not only the moral spirit, but also the relationship with Jesus that motivates us.

The challenge confronting us all today is to rebuild trust, not only in our economy but also in politics and culture as a whole.

> "THE CHALLENGE CONFRONTING ALL OF US TODAY IS TO REBUILD TRUST, NOT ONLY IN OUR ECONOMY BUT ALSO IN POLITICS AND CULTURE AS A WHOLE."

In order to undertake this Herculean task, certain steps must be taken. We need to learn the lessons of what has happened, admit wrongdoing, and work assiduously to deliver the paradigm changes and actions that reflect this new attitude. Trust is rebuilt trade by trade. There is no wholesale way to impart trust: it is built up slowly but surely.

We work on the assumption that we give and receive trust. It's a two-way street. When we go to work, to our offices or wherever, we need both to trust and to be trusted. Trust doesn't happen automatically. We can't just say "trust me" and expect it to happen. It needs an infrastructure. Regulation has a role to play.

There is something that I call "the asymmetry of trust." We expect to receive it but aren't always forthcoming in giving it. With trust we have rights and responsibilities. We have not only the right to receive it but the duty to give it. So we need to keep asking ourselves two questions: To whom do I owe a duty of trust? Do I have a right to receive trust?

There is a temptation from some to see trust as a soft issue. This view sees the statistics as the hard issues and qualitative concepts such as trust as soft. I profoundly disagree. I think it runs to the heart of the financial crisis. Without it, we are in trouble. With it, the market can operate.

Trust, rather, has to do with the way we choose to live our lives, not only in work, but also in our families and communities. Thus, we cannot simply offer "technical" solutions to the economic problems confronting us today.

The reality—the unpalatable reality—is that we, all of us, have a propensity to deviate from the common good. Our inclination is to favor the "me" over the "we"; to prioritize short-term gain over long-term commitment; even to prefer greed over moderation. Clearly, there is an important regulatory role here. However, we should not imagine that regulation in and of itself will cure what Isaiah Berlin called "The crooked timber of humanity."[7] An external support may well correct the worst excess of a tree growing crookedly, but it will be insufficient to straighten it out. Regulation will be helpful—necessary indeed—but it will not deal with the fundamental issue at stake.

The challenge for the financial world in the twenty-first century is to draw a line in the global sand and encourage a more human, and therefore humane, economic vision. Above all, we need to recover a moral spirit that eschews narrow moralizing but recovers a more gracious, less legalistic spirit that recognizes our need for a values-based economy. This is the challenge of our time.

Christians have a distinctive role to play in the reconnecting

> "THE CHALLENGE FOR THE FINANCIAL WORLD IS . . . TO DRAW A LINE IN THE GLOBAL SAND AND ENCOURAGE A MORE HUMAN, AND THEREFORE HUMANE, ECONOMIC VISION."

of the financial and ethical and to ensure that we have a new normal; not merely a hankering after a return to the old days.

It is in embracing this vision that we can rebuild trust in commercial life. We have an extraordinary opportunity before us. If we succeed, we will be creating a better life, not only for ourselves and for those in the poorest parts of our world, but also for future generations. We owe them nothing less.

GOD AT WORK CONVERSATIONS

The *God at Work* conversations are twelve essential short films to inspire the way you work. In this twelve-part series, Ken Costa—in conversation with church leader Pete Hughes—addresses the practical issues facing Christians in the workplace, helping equip people for their unique challenges and opportunities.

You can watch one or more of the conversations on your own or with others, start your own conversation, and transform how your faith impacts your work.

These conversations can be watched on the go, in small groups—as well as in church gatherings for business people. The subjects include:

God's Purpose for Work
Called to Work
Authentically You
Transforming Work Culture
Money Matters

Enjoy Giving
Good Ambition
Failing Well
Right Decisions
Smart Decisions
Living Well
Tackling Stress

Download these free resources at godatwork.org.uk/
conversations.

NOTES

INTRODUCTION

1. "Trust Speech" given by Andrew Haldane, Executive Director, Financial Stability, Bank of England. http://www.bankofengland .co.uk/archive/Documents/historicpubs/speeches/2009/speech 400.pdf.

2. Dennis W. Bakke, *Joy at Work: A Revolutionary Approach to Fun on the Job* (Seattle, WA: PVG, 2005), 19.

3. Ibid., 241–42.

CHAPTER 1: WORK MATTERS

1. Roger Steer, *Hudson Taylor: Lessons in Discipleship* (Oxford: Monarch Books, 1995), 34.

2. http://www.markcazalet.co.uk/index.html.

3. Mark Greene, "The Great Divide", LICC, 2010.

4. William Tyndale, *Doctrinal Treatises and Introductions to Different Portions of the Holy Scriptures*, ed. Henry Walter (Cambridge: The University Press, 1848), 102.

5. Dietrich Bonhoeffer. http://www.goodreads.com/quotes/search ?utf8=✓&q=worldly+bonhoeffer&commit=Search.

CHAPTER 2: WORK AND THE WORLD

1. Walter Brueggemann, *Interpretation and Obedience* (Minneapolis: Fortress, 1991), 199.

2. Walter Isaacson, *Steve Jobs: The Exclusive Biography* (New York: Simon and Schuster, 2011), xxi.

3. http://www.theguardian.com/politics/2010/nov/14/david-cameron-wellbeing-inquiry.

4. Carol Sarler, "It's being so cheerful," *The Sunday Times*, July 30, 2006. http://www.newenglishreview.org/blog_direct_link.cfm/blog_id/1144/Its-being-so-cheerful-as-keeps-me-going.

5. www.johnlewispartnership.co.uk/about/our-principles.html.

6. William James, *The Varieties of Religious Experience* (New York: Random House, 1902), 77.

7. Immanuel Kant, *Groundwork for the Metaphysics of Morals*, ed. Lara Denis (Peterborough, Ontario: Broadview Editions, 2005), 78.

8. Oliver James, *Affluenza: How to Be Successful and Stay Sane* (London: Vermilion, 2007).

9. See www.prosperity.com and www.li.com.

10. Oliver Burkeman, "Bill Gates: I Don't Want to Be the World's Richest Man." http://www.theguardian.com/media/2006/may/05/citynews.digitalmedia.

CHAPTER 3: AMBITION AND LIFE CHOICES

1. http://www.deppimpact.com/about_himself.php.

2. Radiohead song "Paranoid Android".

3. http://www.telegraph.co.uk/finance/2850002/Business-Profile-Plenty-of-room-to-be-content.html.

4. Roy Hattersley, *Blood and Fire: William and Catherine Booth and the Salvation Army* (London: Abacus, 2000).

5. *The Times* (London). September 26, 2005. Sphttps://books.google .co.uk/books?id=-TczBQAAQBAJ&pg=PT7048&lpg=PT7048& dq=jean-pierre+garnier+passionate+and+unsuccessful&source =bl&ots=sfI38GNgdt&sig=m0cGaAikpqQvsmtJtUFKE-ozfz8& hl=en&sa=X&ved=0ahUKEwiA-_KHq4vMAhUE9g4KHZS0Awc Q6AEIHzAB#v=onepage&q=jean-pierre&f=false.

6. John Adair, *Develop Your Leadership Skills* (London: Kogan Page, 2007), 53. https://books.google.co.uk/books?id=BYMWl2FEK28 C&pg=PA56&lpg=PA56&dq.

7. *Chariots of Fire*, directed by Hugh Hudson, Twentieth Century Fox Film Corporation, 1981.

8. http://www.julietwest.com/.

9. Stephen Covey, *The Seven Habits of Highly Effective People: Powerful Lessons in Personal Change* (New York: Simon & Schuster, 2013).

10. William Shakespeare, *Henry VIII*, 3.2.528.

CHAPTER 4: TOUGH DECISIONS

1. Kim Paffenroth, *Augustine and Liberal Education* (Plymouth, UK: Lexington Books, 2008), page 90. https://books.google.co .uk/books?id=n996M7-1eosC&pg=PA90&lpg=PA90&dq= augustine+silent+clamour+of+truth&source=bl&ots=9_uUrvh 7tr&sig=LRfS8WOFLOnJ292M20ThSYxrc_o&hl=en&sa=X& ved=0ahUKEwjxmYmfsIvMAhWFjQ8KHf0sDLcQ6AEIHTAA #v=onepage&q=augustine%20silent%20clamour%20of%20truth &f=false.

2. *The Message.*

3. Colonel Red Reeder, *Omar Nelson Bradley, the Soldiers' General* (Champaign, IL: Garrard Publishing, 2011).

4. In conversation with Siegmund Warburg.

CHAPTER 5: WORK-LIFE BALANCE

1. Arnold Bennett, *How to Live on 24 Hours a Day* (New Zealand: Aeterna, 2009).

2. http://archive.fortune.com/magazines/fortune/fortune_archive /2002/11/18/332268/index.htm.

3. *The Times* (London). September 26, 2005. Sphttps://books.google .co.uk/books?id=-TczBQAAQBAJ&pg=PT7048&lpg=PT7048&dq =jean-pierre+garnier+passionate+and+unsuccessful&source=bl& ots=sfI38GNgdt&sig=m0cGaAikpqQvsmtJtUFKE-ozfz8&hl=en &sa=X&ved=0ahUKEwiA-_KHq4vMAhUE9g4KHZS0AwcQ6AE IHzAB#v=onepage&q=jean-pierre&f=false.

CHAPTER 6: STRESS

1. http://journals.lww.com/psychosomaticmedicine/Abstract/1998 /11000/A_Longitudinal_Study_of_Job_Strain_and_Ambulatory.7.aspx.

2. See www.isma.org.uk/about-stress/facts-about-stress.

3. 2005 *Guardian* interview with psychoanalyst Adam Phillips about his book, *Going Sane*: www.guardian.co.uk/books/2005/ feb/13/booksonhealth.lifeandhealth.

4. John Milton, *Paradise Lost* (London: Whittaker, Treacher, & Co., 1832), 8.

5. *NIV Bible in One Year*, Hodder & Stoughton, 2011. To receive a free daily e-mail, which includes daily readings and thoughts from Nicky and Pippa Gumbel, or to download the free Bible in One Year app, visit htb.org.uk.

6. https://www.godatwork.org.uk/sites/godatwork.org/files /ConversationStarters_BookletFINAL.pdf.

CHAPTER 7: FAILURE, DISAPPOINTMENT, AND HOPE

1. https://issuu.com/alphaindia/docs/100718b_alphaindianews
   _july2010_web.

2. Thom Winckelmann and Lynn Abushanab, *Bono: Rock Star & Humanitarian* (Edina, MN: ABDO Publishing, 2010), 19. https://books.google.co.uk/books?id=jXtGsci7XIAC&pg=PA19&lpg=PA19&dq=bono+don%27t+dream+to+dream+is+to+be+disappointed&source=bl&ots=w5KznkVOYm&sig=Vzjp6PIw6YcE6tuDOEbnWr8PnCs&hl=en&sa=X&ved=0ahUKEwjA477M84vMAhVIcBoKHbfZCpsQ6AEIJTAC#v=onepage&q=bono%20don't%20dream%20to%20dream%20is%20to%20be%20disappointed&f=false.

3. John Mark Comer, *Garden City: Work, Rest, and the Art of Being Human* (Grand Rapids, MI: Zondervan, 2015).

CHAPTER 8: MONEY AND GIVING

1. Guy de Rothschild, *Whims of Fortune: The Memoirs of Guy de Rothschild* (New York: Random House, 1985).

2. http://www.managementtoday.co.uk/news/661226/%20sir%20nigel%20rudd%20profile.

3. http://www.christianpost.com/news/the-third-conversion-121761/.

4. http://wesley.nnu.edu/john-wesley/the-sermons-of-john-wesley-1872-edition/sermon-50-the-use-of-money/.

CHAPTER 9: SPIRITUAL RENEWAL

1. World Economc Forum, Davos, Switzerland, January 26, 2001. http://fox.presidencia.gob.mx/actividades/?contenido=473.

2. http://www.telegraph.co.uk/news/uknews/1503072/Queen-extols-the-unique-power-of-Christianity.html.

3. Andy Crouch, *Playing God: Redeeming the Gift of Power* (Downers Grove, IL: InterVarsity Press, 2013), 91.

4. http://www.bbcamerica.com/anglophenia/2013/03/the-wit-and -wisdom-of-michael-caine.

5. *Junebug*, directed by Phil Morrison, 2005 (Culver City, CA: Sony Pictures Home Entertainment, 2006), DVD.

AFTERMATH: THE MORAL SPIRIT IN LIGHT OF THE FINANCIAL CRISIS

1. http://www.telegraph.co.uk/news/uknews/theroyalfamily/3386353 /The-Queen-asks-why-no-one-saw-the-credit-crunch-coming.html.

2. T. S. Eliot, *The Rock: A Pageant Play Written for Performance on Behalf of the Forth-Five Churches Fund of the Diocese of London* (London: Faber & Faber, 1934).

3. http://www.bbc.co.uk/programmes/b00kt7rg.

4. World Economic Forum, Davos, Switzerland, January 2009. http://news.bbc.co.uk/2/hi/business/davos/7860761.stm.

5. P. Hyde and B. Williamson, "The Importance of Organisational Values," *Focus on Change Management*, 66, 2000, pp. 14–18.

6. R. van Lee, L. Fabish, and N. Gaw, *The Value of Corporate Values: Strategy and Business Issues* (Washington, D.C.: Booz Allen Hamilton/Aspen Institute, 2006).

7. http://press.princeton.edu/chapters/s9983.pdf.

ABOUT THE AUTHOR

KEN COSTA IS AN INTERNATIONALLY RENOWNED BANKER, HAVING worked as chairman of UBS Investment Bank for EMEA and chairman of Lazard International. He is the chairman of Alpha International, emeritus professor of commerce in Gresham College London, dean of the Leadership College London, and author of *Know Your Why*. He and his wife, Dr. Fiona Costa, live in London. They have two sons and two daughters.

ALSO AVAILABLE FROM

KEN COSTA

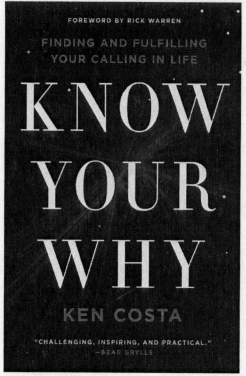

ISBN 9780718087715

AVAILABLE WHEREVER BOOKS AND EBOOKS ARE SOLD

W Publishing Group

An Imprint of Thomas Nelson